ELM TREE BOOKS

Cookery Editor
Mary Pope

Production Editor
Joan Durrant

Design
Bryan Austin Associates Ltd

Copyright 1979 Standbrook Publications Ltd,
a member of the Thomson Organisation

Distributed to the book trade by Elm Tree Books/Hamish Hamilton Ltd,
Garden House, 57/59 Long Acre, London WC2E 9JZ

ISBN 0 241 10390 8

Printed by Sackville Press Billericay Limited,
Radford Way, Billericay, Essex CM12 0BZ

Contents

On the cover: Coffee Layer Cake, recipe on page 26

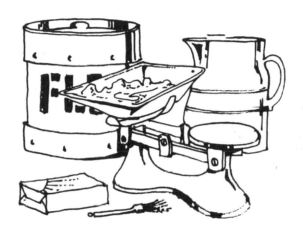

Introduction

Following the success of our first LIVING cake book –
Cakes, Biscuits and Bakes – we here present a second one,
which we hope you will like just as much.

Like the first, it is a collection of recipes originally published
in LIVING magazine, but with some exciting new ones,
too. And in this new book, there is a larger selection of gâteaux
and dessert cakes. This, we think, follows a trend in
cake-making, which perhaps reflects the way we live now.

Afternoon tea is a less usual happening, so the kind of
cake that can either be served as a sweet course for a lunch or
dinner party, or at a tea party, has come into its own. But
of course, we also give you all the old tested and tried,
favourite kinds of cakes and bakes.

Baking in Brief

Equipment

You'll need: *mixing bowls, wooden spoons, chopping board, electric or wire whisk, large metal spoon with cutting edge for 'folding-in', pastry brushes, spatula, palette knife, wire cooling rack,* and a *plastic ruler* for measuring tins, etc, is a useful extra.

In this book, a teaspoon is a *5 ml spoon*, a tablespoon is a *15 ml spoon*.

Make sure you have these sizes. A *measuring jug* is essential and good *scales*.

Cake and sandwich tins should be in appropriate sizes. A 20 cm (8in) round tin holds the same amount as an 18 cm (7in) square tin – amounts increase in ratio.

Loaf tins vary in size, so in this book we have given liquid capacities.

When your tin has not the exact capacity needed, choose a bigger size – but in this case your cake may cook more quickly.

Oven temperatures do vary, so get to know your own oven and adjust when necessary.

Get everything ready before starting work. Grease and line tins – non-stick paper is available. Have all ingredients at room temperature and warm your bowl.

Whisked sponges: Whisk eggs and sugar over hot water until the mixture will hold the trail of the whisk when it is lifted. Fold in the sifted flour – never stir it in. The aim is to fold air into the mixture, and make it really light and spongy. Don't keep your sponge waiting once it is made. Into the tin and into the oven!

6

Creamed mixtures: Do not over-cream *soft margarine*. Do cream *butter* for some time – it must look light and fluffy.

Treat unfamiliar spices and flavourings with caution. Begin with a quarter or half quantity.

Storage: Most cakes and biscuits will keep well for up to a week in an airtight container in a cool place. Some richer, moister cakes improve with keeping.

Bread

Fresh yeast should be stored in a screwtop jar, a plastic container with a snap-fitting lid, or a polythene bag. It will keep for 4-5 days in a cool larder, 1-2 weeks in a refrigerator, up to 6 months in a freezer. See notes about *dried yeast* on page 60, and *kneading* (in recipe for Quick Yorkshire teacakes) on page 62.

Rising: Put dough to rise over a cooker (but not over a pilot light or other direct heat) with the oven heated to lowest setting, or put it over a radiator.

Using an electric mixer: If using electricity for *whisked mixtures*, it is not necessary to whisk over hot water. Warm the mixer bowl. For *creamed mixtures*, cream butter and sugar and beat in eggs by electricity, but fold in flour by hand. Do not use electricity for soft margarine.

Freezing

Most cakes and bakes freeze well. The normal rules of careful wrapping and fast-freezing apply, and short storage times usually give best results. *Decorated cakes* should be open-frozen until solid before wrapping. *Icings* (apart from glacé icing) freeze well, so do butter icing fillings, but avoid jam and cream. Usually it is best to freeze sandwich cakes unfilled and fill after thawing.

chapter 1
Fruit Cakes

Here are the fruit cakes, from the plain family one to the rich birthday or wedding cake – plus some more unusual recipes made with ingredients like honey, pineapple, ripe plums, apricots, fruit salad, brazil nuts and black cherry jam

PLAIN FRUIT CAKE

(Cuts into 12 slices)
150 g (5oz) soft margarine
150 g (5oz) castor sugar
2 eggs
275 g (10oz) mixed dried fruit
225 g (8oz) self-raising flour
1 level teaspoon mixed spice
100 ml (4fl oz) milk

1 Preheat a cool oven (150 deg C, 300 deg F, Gas 2), centre shelf. Brush an 18 cm (7in) round cake tin with oil, and line it with greased greaseproof paper.
2 Put all the ingredients together into a mixing bowl, and stir well until the mixture is blended to a soft dropping consistency.
3 Turn into the prepared tin, and smooth the top. Bake for 2 hours, until firm to the touch.
4 Turn out and cool on a wire rack.

FRUIT SALAD CAKE

(Cuts into 12 slices)
450 g (1lb) dried fruit salad (soaked in advance in cold tea)
150 ml (5fl oz) cold tea
175 g (6oz) butter or margarine
175 g (6oz) castor sugar
2 large eggs
225 g (8oz) self-raising flour
1 level teaspoon mixed spice
½ level teaspoon cinnamon
icing sugar for dredging

1 Chop the fruit coarsely, place in a bowl. Pour over the cold tea and leave to soak for 24 hours. Stir the fruit occasionally.
2 Preheat a cool oven (150 deg C, 300 deg F, Gas 2), shelf below centre. Grease a 20 cm (8in) round cake tin and line with greased greaseproof paper.
3 Cream the butter and sugar until soft and light. Whisk the eggs, gradually beat into the creamed mixture.
4 Sift the flour with the spices. Fold into the mixture using a metal spoon. Add the soaked fruit salad and mix.
5 Turn the mixture into the prepared tin. Smooth over the top and make a slight hollow in the centre.
6 Bake for 2¼-2½ hours or until well browned and firm to the touch.
7 Turn out of the tin when cool and dredge the top with icing sugar.

*It is important to follow **either** the metric **or** the imperial weights and measures in any one recipe*

HONEY FRUIT CAKE

(Cuts into 10 slices)
225 g (8oz) butter, slightly softened
225 g (8oz) honey
3 eggs, lightly beaten
225 g (8oz) plain flour
2 level tablespoons self-raising flour
pinch of salt
¼ level teaspoon nutmeg
¼ level teaspoon mixed spice
100 g (4oz) dried apricots
50 g (2oz) raisins
50 g (2oz) currants
50 g (2oz) chopped mixed peel
50 g (2oz) chopped almonds
⅛ level teaspoon bicarbonate of soda
2 teaspoons hot water

1 Preheat a moderately hot oven (200 deg C, 400 deg F, Gas 6), centre shelf. Grease an 18 cm (7in) round cake tin, and line it with a double layer of greased greaseproof paper.
2 Cream the butter and honey, beat in the eggs one at a time, adding a little plain flour after each one.
3 Sift flours together with the salt and spices and fold in.
4 Chop the apricots; fold into the mixture with the other fruit, peel and nuts.
5 Dissolve the bicarbonate of soda in the hot water and stir in.
6 Put into the cake tin, level the top and bake for 20 minutes. Reduce the oven temperature to warm (170 deg C, 325 deg F, Gas 3) and cook for a further 1 hour 20 minutes, or until a skewer inserted in the centre comes out clean.
7 Leave to cool in the tin, then remove from the tin and take off the paper.

SEMI RICH FRUIT CAKE

(Makes one 18cm/7in square cake)
225 g (8oz) margarine
175 g (6oz) castor sugar
3 large eggs
¼ teaspoon vanilla essence
350 g (12oz) plain flour
2 level teaspoons baking powder
¼ level teaspoon mixed spice
pinch of salt
100 g (4oz) chopped mixed peel
100 g (4oz) glacé cherries, halved
100 g (4oz) chopped dates
150 ml (5fl oz) cold tea

1 Preheat a warm oven (170 deg C, 325 deg F, Gas 3), centre shelf. Grease an 18 cm (7in) square cake tin and line with greased greaseproof paper.
2 Cream the margarine and sugar until light and fluffy.

3 Gradually beat in the eggs, one at a time, and the vanilla essence.
4 Sift together the flour, the baking powder, mixed spice and salt.
5 Fold the flour mixture and prepared fruits alternately into the creamed mixture and gradually add the tea. It should be a fairly moist mixture.
6 Place in the prepared tin, level the surface and slightly hollow out the centre.
7 Cook for about 2 hours until a fine skewer inserted in the centre comes out clean.
8 Cool in the tin before removing paper.

RICH FRUIT CAKE

(Makes one 23 cm/9in round or 20 cm/8in square cake)
225 g (8oz) butter
225 g (8oz) soft rich brown sugar
4 eggs
225 g (8oz) plain flour
¼ level teaspoon salt
1 level teaspoon mixed spice
350 g (12oz) seedless raisins
350 g (12oz) currants
125 g (4oz) sultanas
125 g (4oz) chopped mixed peel
125 g (4oz) glacé cherries
50 g (2oz) chopped almonds or walnuts
grated rind 1 orange
grated rind 1 lemon
3 tablespoons brandy, rum, whisky or milk

1 Preheat a very cool oven (140 deg C, 275 deg F, Gas 1), centre shelf. Grease a 23 cm (9in) round or 20 cm (8in) square cake tin and line it with greased greaseproof paper.
2 In a large mixing bowl, cream the butter and sugar together until light and fluffy. Gradually beat in the eggs, beating well after each addition.
3 Sift in the flour, salt and mixed spice and add remaining ingredients. Mix thoroughly.
4 Turn the mixture into the prepared tin and level the surface. The cake can be left to stand in a cool place overnight before baking – if left in the refrigerator allow the cake to return to room temperature before baking.
5 Bake for about 3½-4 hours. The cake is cooked when a skewer inserted in the centre comes out clean. As oven thermostats do vary, check after 2 hours that the top is not over-browning – if necessary cover the top of the tin with a piece of paper.
6 Cool the cake in the tin. When cold remove from the tin and wrap in greaseproof paper and then foil. Keep for at least one month before serving.

Note: *This cake is suitable to use as the base for birthday and wedding cakes. If liked, the cooled cake can be sprinkled with 2 tablespoons brandy, rum or whisky before wrapping. Royal icing, apricot glaze and almond paste recipes are on pages 80-81.*

9

SUGARED FRUIT AND GINGER CAKE

(Cuts into 16 slices)
50 g (2oz) glacé cherries
100 g (4oz) preserved stem ginger in syrup
25 g (1oz) crystallised pineapple
225 g (8oz) self-raising flour
¼ level teaspoon salt
1 level teaspoon ground ginger
150 g (5oz) butter or margarine
125 g (4oz) soft brown sugar
2 large eggs
25 g (1oz) chopped mixed peel
50 g (2oz) raisins
75 g (3oz) icing sugar

1 Preheat a warm oven (170 deg C, 325 deg F, Gas 3), centre shelf. Grease a 20 cm (8in) round cake tin and line with greased greaseproof paper.
2 Rinse the glacé cherries and stem ginger under running hot water. Dry and quarter the cherries. Chop the pineapple. Chop all but one piece of the stem ginger and toss lightly in a little of the flour.
3 Sift the flour, salt and ground ginger. Cream the butter and sugar together until pale and fluffy.
4 Beat the eggs, then a little at a time beat them into the creamed mixture, beating well after each addition.
5 Fold in half the sifted flour, then the cherries, pineapple, chopped ginger, mixed peel, raisins. Fold in remaining flour, turn the mixture into the tin, level the surface.
6 Bake for about 1¼ hours until well risen and firm to touch. Cool in tin, turn on to wire rack, remove paper.
7 Chop the remaining ginger.
8 Measure 2 tablespoons of syrup from the ginger into a saucepan, add the icing sugar and stir over a medium heat until smoothly blended and just warm. Add the ginger. Quickly spread over the top of the cold cake and let it trickle down the sides; put aside to set.

See picture opposite

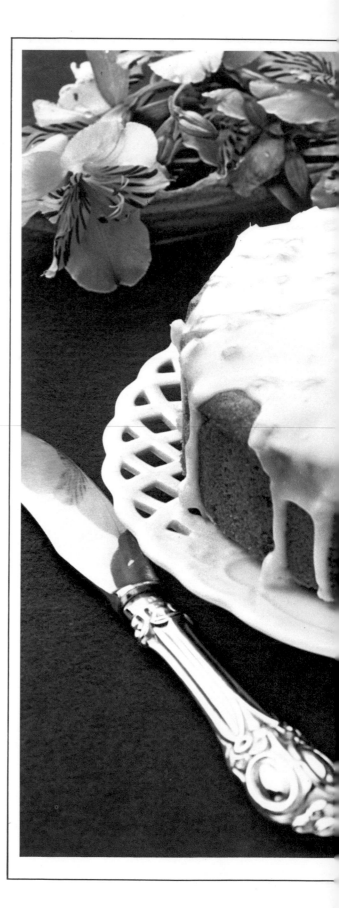

Sugared Fruit and Ginger Cake, *see opposite*

GRANNY'S FRUIT CAKE

(Makes one 20 cm/8in cake)
150 g (5oz) plain flour
pinch of salt
1 level teaspoon baking powder
1 level teaspoon mixed spice
125 g (5oz) wholewheat flour
100 g (4oz) currants
100 g (4oz) sultanas
100 g (4oz) seedless raisins
50 g (2oz) chopped mixed peel
50 g (2oz) blanched almonds, finely chopped
100 g (4oz) glacé cherries
finely grated rind 1 lemon
225 g (8oz) butter or margarine
225 g (8oz) soft brown sugar
4 eggs
a little milk if necessary

1 Preheat a warm oven (170 deg C, 325 deg F, Gas 3), shelf below centre. Grease a 20 cm (8in) round cake tin, and line with greased greaseproof paper.
2 Sift the plain flour, salt, baking powder and mixed spice into a bowl. Stir in the wholewheat flour, dried fruits, peel and almonds. Chop half the cherries and add with the lemon rind.
3 Put the butter and sugar in a bowl and cream together until soft. Beat in the eggs, one at a time, beating well after each addition.
4 Fold half the flour and fruit mixture into the creamed mixture and, when thoroughly combined, fold in the remainder. Add a little milk if needed; the mixture should drop off the spoon when shaken.
5 Transfer to the tin and level the top. Cut the remaining glacé cherries in half and arrange on the top.
6 Bake for about 2½ hours or until a skewer inserted in the centre comes out clean.
7 Cool in the tin for 10-15 minutes, discard the grease-proof paper and leave the cake on a wire rack until cold.
Note: *This keeps well in an airtight container up to 2 weeks.*

IRISH FRUIT CAKE

(Makes one 18 cm/7in cake)
450 g (1lb) mixed dried fruit
5 tablespoons Guinness
175 g (6oz) butter or margarine
175 g (6oz) castor sugar
3 eggs
175 g (6oz) plain flour
50 g (2oz) self-raising flour
1-2 level teaspoons ground mixed spice
1 level tablespoon granulated sugar

1 Leave mixed dried fruit to soak in the Guinness for 2 hours, stirring occasionally.
2 Preheat a moderate oven (180 deg C, 350 deg F, Gas 4), centre shelf. Grease an 18 cm (7in) round cake tin and line with greased greaseproof paper.
3 Cream the butter and castor sugar until soft and pale. Beat in the eggs gradually, beating well after each addition. Sift the flours and spice (to taste) together, then fold into the creamed mixture with the soaked fruit and any remaining Guinness.
4 Spoon into the prepared tin, level the surface, sprinkle with granulated sugar.
5 Bake for 1½ hours until firm in the centre. Cool in the tin for 5 minutes before turning out. Remove the paper, cool on a wire rack.
Note: *This keeps well in an airtight container up to 2 weeks.*

BLACK BUN

(Cuts into 12 slices)
PASTRY
450 g (1lb) frozen shortcrust pastry, thawed; or home-made shortcrust made with 275 g (10oz) plain flour, etc
CAKE FILLING
125 g (4oz) plain flour
pinch of salt
¼ level teaspoon baking powder
⅛ level teaspoon ground black pepper
½ level teaspoon ground ginger
½ level teaspoon ground cinnamon
50 g (2oz) soft brown sugar
225 g (8oz) seedless or stoned raisins
225 g (8oz) currants
25 g (1oz) chopped mixed peel
25 g (1oz) chopped almonds
1 small cooking apple, peeled, cored and grated
1 egg beaten with 1 tablespoon milk

1 Preheat a warm oven (170 deg C, 325 deg F, Gas 3), centre shelf. Have ready either a 15 cm (6in) square or an 18 cm (7in) round, deep cake tin.
2 Roll out three-quarters of the shortcrust pastry to a size which will fit over the base and up the sides of the selected tin, leaving about 2 cm (1in) overlapping the edge. Ease neatly into the tin.
3 **To make the cake filling:** Sift the flour, salt, baking powder, ground black pepper, ground ginger and cinnamon into a mixing bowl. Stir in the sugar, raisins, currants, the chopped mixed peel, chopped almonds and the grated apple.
4 Add the beaten egg and milk, mix to a stiff mixture. Turn into the pastry lined tin, press down.
5 Roll the remaining pastry to the size of the top of the tin, trim and put on top of cake mixture.
6 Trim the overlapping pastry leaving 1 cm (½in); brush with water and fold over on to the pastry top. Seal edges together firmly, using the prongs of a fork.
7 Make several holes in the pastry lid with a skewer. Brush the top with milk.
8 Bake for 2 hours or until a skewer inserted in the centre comes out clean. Turn out.
9 When cold, store in an airtight container for at least a week before serving.

FAMILY DATE, ORANGE AND WALNUT CAKE

(Cuts into 12 slices)
350 g (12oz) plain flour
1½ level teaspoons baking powder
¼ level teaspoon salt
175 g (6oz) demerara sugar
175 g (6oz) butter or margarine
100 g (4oz) cooking dates, chopped
50 g (2oz) walnut pieces, chopped
grated rind 1 orange
2 eggs
150 ml (5fl oz) milk

1 Preheat a moderate oven (180 deg C, 350 deg F, Gas 4), centre shelf. Grease a 2-litre (3½-pint) loaf tin and line with greased greaseproof paper.
2 Sift the flour, baking powder, salt and sugar into a mixing bowl and cut in the butter.
3 Rub the fat into the mixture until it resembles fine breadcrumbs, then stir in the chopped nuts, dates and orange rind.
4 Beat the eggs, mix into the dry ingredients with sufficient milk to give a dropping consistency.
5 Turn the mixture into the prepared tin, level the surface. Bake 1¼-1½ hours, until the centre feels firm.
6 Leave the cake to cool.

FRUITY WHOLEMEAL CAKE

(Cuts into 10 slices)
275 g (10oz) wholemeal flour
pinch of salt
1 level teaspoon baking powder
½ level teaspoon ground cinnamon
100 g (4oz) margarine
75 g (3oz) sultanas
25 g (1oz) glacé cherries, quartered
25 g (1oz) chopped mixed peel
100 g (4oz) castor sugar
2 large eggs
6 tablespoons milk
25 g (1oz) chocolate drops for cooking (optional)

1 Preheat a moderate oven (180 deg C, 350 deg F, Gas 4), shelf below centre. Lightly grease an 18 cm (7in) round cake tin.
2 Sift the flour, salt, baking powder and cinnamon into a bowl. Add the margarine and rub in well.
3 Stir in the sultanas, glacé cherries, peel and sugar.
4 Beat the eggs and milk together; mix into the dry ingredients to make a fairly soft consistency.
5 Place the mixture in the tin, smooth the surface, sprinkle with the chocolate drops (if using). Cook for one hour until a thin skewer inserted in the centre comes out quite clean.
6 Cool in the tin for 10 minutes, then on a wire rack.

CHERRY AND BRAZIL NUT CAKE

(Cuts into about 10 slices)
100 g (4oz) margarine
100 g (4oz) castor sugar
2 eggs
2 tablespoons milk
1 teaspoon lemon juice
150 g (6oz) self-raising flour
pinch of salt
finely grated rind ½ lemon
50 g (2oz) glacé cherries, quartered
50 g (2oz) shelled brazil nuts, chopped
TOPPING (optional)
2 tablespoons apricot jam
1 level teaspoon chopped brazil nuts

1 Preheat a warm oven (170 deg C, 325 deg F, Gas 3), centre shelf. Grease a 15 cm (6in) round cake tin and line with greased greaseproof paper.
2 Beat the margarine and sugar together in a bowl until creamy. Beat in the eggs, milk and lemon juice.
3 Using a metal spoon, gradually fold in the flour, salt, lemon rind, cherries and brazil nuts.
4 Place in the cake tin and cook for about 1 hour 20 minutes, until light pressure with the fingers leaves no mark. Leave to cool slightly in the tin before turning out on to a wire rack to finish cooling.
5 **To make the topping:** If liked, cover the top of the cake with hot sieved jam and sprinkle the edge with nuts.

BLACK CHERRY CAKE

(Cuts into 10-12 slices)
125 g (4oz) butter or margarine
125 g (4oz) castor sugar
2 eggs
a few drops almond essence
225 g (8oz) self-raising flour, sifted
4 level tablespoons black cherry jam
1 level tablespoon castor sugar

1 Preheat a warm oven (170 deg C, 325 deg F, Gas 3), centre shelf. Brush a 16-18 cm (6½-7in) round cake tin with oil and line with greased greaseproof paper.
2 Cream the butter and sugar together in a mixing bowl, until pale and fluffy.
3 Beat the eggs, add the almond essence, and gradually beat into the creamed mixture. Fold in the flour.
4 Add the jam, stirring carefully to distribute the fruit evenly in the mixture.
5 Turn into the prepared tin, smooth over the top and sprinkle with castor sugar.
6 Bake for 1 hour 10 minutes, until well risen and golden. Turn out on a wire rack to cool.

Note: *Any full fruit jam can be used in this cake, eg apricot, strawberry, blackcurrant.*

13

GERMAN PLUM CAKE

(Cuts into 8 pieces)
175 g (6oz) plain flour
½ level teaspoon baking powder
½ level teaspoon salt
1 level teaspoon finely grated lemon rind
50 g (2oz) castor sugar
85 g (3½oz) butter or margarine
1 egg, beaten
milk
2 level tablespoons ground almonds
1 kg (2lb) black dessert plums, halved and stoned
2-3 level tablespoons castor sugar for sprinkling

1 Preheat a moderately hot oven (200 deg C, 400 deg F, Gas 6), shelf above centre.
2 Well grease an oblong tin, 25 cm by 20 cm by 5 cm (10in by 8in by 2in).
3 Sift the flour, baking powder and salt into a bowl. Add the lemon rind and sugar.
4 Rub in the butter, mix to a fairly stiff dough with beaten egg. Gather together and press evenly over the base of the tin.
5 Brush with milk, sprinkle with almonds then cover closely with rows of halved plums, cut sides up.
6 Bake for ½ hour till the base is cooked. Remove from the oven, sprinkle the plums with sugar, cool slightly.
7 Cut into about 8 pieces, serve with with cream if liked. Serve the day it is made.

APRICOT FRUIT CAKE

(Cuts into 12 slices)
225 g (8oz) dried apricots, washed and chopped
275 ml (½ pint) water
275 g (10oz) margarine
225 g (8oz) sultanas
113 g (4oz) carton mixed peel
1 large size can condensed milk
grated rind 2 lemons
50 g (2oz) ground almonds
¾ level teaspoon bicarbonate of soda
275 g (10oz) plain flour, sifted
pinch of salt
25 g (1oz) blanched almonds, split lengthwise

1 Soak the apricots in the water for ½ hour.
2 Preheat a warm oven (170 deg C, 325 deg F, Gas 3), centre shelf. Grease a 20 cm (8in) round cake tin and line with greased double greaseproof paper.
3 Place the apricots and the water in a fairly large saucepan.
4 Add the margarine, sultanas, mixed peel, condensed milk, lemon rind and ground almonds. Heat gently to melt the margarine, then bring to the boil, stirring all the time. Reduce heat and simmer for 3 minutes.
5 Remove pan from the heat and allow to cool.
6 Quickly stir in the bicarbonate of soda and fold in the flour and salt at once.
7 Place in the prepared cake tin, level the surface and arrange the halved almonds over the top.
8 Cook for 1¾ hours, then cover the cake with a double layer of greaseproof paper and cook for a further hour. The cake is cooked when a fine skewer inserted through the centre comes out clean.

See picture opposite

14

Apricot Fruit Cake, *see opposite;* **Orange Caraway Buns,** *page 48;* **Walnut and Date Teabread,** *page 68;* **Gingernuts,** *page 52*

chapter 2
Family Cakes

The lighter cakes – the whisked sponges and rolls, the creamed sandwiches and layer cakes, deliciously flavoured with fruit juices, nuts, spices – take your choice

ALMOND CARROT CAKE

(Cuts into 10-12 slices)
175 g (6oz) plain flour
1½ level teaspoons bicarbonate of soda
1 level teaspoon salt
2 level teaspoons ground cinnamon
125 g (4oz) wholemeal flour
200 g (8oz) grated carrot
125 g (4oz) chopped almonds
3 large eggs
225 g (8oz) granulated sugar
175 ml (6fl oz) oil
BUTTER ICING
75 g (3oz) butter
150 g (6oz) icing sugar
1 teaspoon lemon juice
extra icing sugar for dredging

1 Preheat a moderate oven (180 deg C, 350 deg F, Gas 4), centre shelf.
2 Grease and flour two 20 cm (8in) square or round sandwich tins.
3 Sift the plain flour with the bicarbonate of soda, salt and spice into a bowl. Mix in the wholemeal flour, grated carrot and almonds.
4 Place the eggs in a large bowl, beat well. Add the sugar and oil and beat together. Add the flour mixture and stir with a wooden spoon until well mixed.
5 Turn into the prepared tins. Bake for 50-60 minutes until evenly browned, and a metal skewer inserted in the centre comes out clean.
6 Turn out and cool on a wire rack.
7 **To make the butter icing:** Place the butter in a medium-sized bowl and cream until soft. Sift in the icing sugar and beat together until soft and light. Mix in the lemon juice.
8 Sandwich the cake together with butter icing. Dredge the top with icing sugar.

LEMON AND ALMOND CAKE

(Makes one 19 cm/7½in cake)
175 g (6oz) butter or margarine
175 g (6oz) castor sugar
3 eggs, beaten
about 50 g (2oz) lemon curd
finely grated rind ½ large lemon
a few drops almond essence
50 g (2oz) ground almonds
175 (6oz) self-raising flour
25 g (1oz) flaked almonds

1 Preheat a warm oven (170 deg C, 325 deg F, Gas 3), centre shelf. Grease a 19 cm (7½in) round cake tin and line with greased greaseproof paper.
2 Cream the butter and sugar until soft and pale. Gradually beat in the eggs, then the lemon curd, lemon rind and almond essence. Fold in the ground almonds and flour until evenly mixed.
3 Turn the mixture into the prepared tin, level the surface and sprinkle thickly with flaked almonds. Bake for 1-1¼ hours until lightly browned and when a skewer inserted in the centre comes out clean.
4 Cool in the tin 5 minutes then turn out carefully and remove the paper. Cool on a wire rack.

Note: *This is quite a moist cake so don't worry if it sinks a little in the centre. Keeps well in airtight container up to one week.*

*It is important to follow **either** the metric **or** the imperial weights and measures in any one recipe*

SESAME SEED CAKE

(Makes one 20 cm/8in cake)

225 g (8oz) butter or margarine
375 g (13oz) castor sugar
5 eggs, beaten
225 g (8oz) plain flour
few drops vanilla essence
pinch of salt
2-3 level teaspoons sesame seeds

1 Preheat a warm oven (170 deg C, 325 deg F, Gas 3), centre shelf. Grease and flour a 20 cm (8in) round cake tin.
2 Cream the butter and sugar until light and fluffy. Gradually beat in the eggs, beating well after each addition and adding 2 tablespoons of the flour with the last egg. Stir in the vanilla essence.
3 Sift in the flour and salt, add 2 teaspoons sesame seeds and mix well until evenly blended.
4 Turn into the tin and level the surface. Sprinkle, if liked, with remaining sesame seeds.
5 Bake for 1½-1¾ hours until a skewer inserted in the centre comes out clean.
6 Cool on a wire rack. The cake improves in texture and flavour if kept for 1-2 days before serving.

LEMON AND SPICE LAYER CAKE

(Makes one 20 cm/8in cake)

175 g (6oz) butter or margarine
175 g (6oz) soft brown sugar
3 eggs, beaten
200 g (7oz) self-raising flour
1 level teaspoon mixed spice
1 level teaspoon instant coffee powder
1 tablespoon warm water
225 g (8oz) almond paste, bought or home-made
3 rounded tablespoons lemon curd
100 g (4oz) icing sugar, sifted
1-2 tablespoons lemon juice
yellow food colouring
crystallised lemon slices (optional)

1 Preheat a moderate oven (180 deg C, 350 deg F, Gas 4), shelf above centre. Grease a 20 cm (8in) round cake tin and line the base with greased greaseproof paper.
2 Cream the butter and sugar until light and fluffy, gradually beat in the eggs.
3 Sift the flour, spice and coffee together, then mix half into the creamed mixture, add a tablespoon warm water then fold in the remaining flour.
4 Turn the mixture into the tin and level the surface. Bake for about 50 minutes until well risen and firm to the touch. Turn the cake out, remove paper and cool on a wire rack.
5 Halve the almond paste, roll into 20 cm (8in) rounds.

6 Cut the cold cake into 3 equal layers, sandwich them together with lemon curd and the almond paste rounds.
7 Mix the icing sugar with sufficient lemon juice to make a fairly thick smooth icing.
8 Twist a small rectangle of greaseproof paper into a firm cone, fold the top loose edges together to secure.
9 Place 2 teaspoons of icing into this piping bag and snip off bottom to make a fine hole.
10 Colour the remaining icing yellow and spread it over the top of the cake. Quickly pipe lines of the white icing, about 2 cm (1in) apart, across the cake. Then lightly drag the tip of a skewer across the lines, first one way then the other, to give a feathered effect.
11 Decorate round edge with crystallised lemon slices.

LAYERED COCONUT ORANGE SLICE

(Cuts into 12 slices)

175 g (6oz) butter or margarine
175 g (6oz) castor sugar
3 eggs, beaten
grated rind 1 orange
175 g (6oz) self-raising flour
50 g (2oz) desiccated coconut
2 tablespoons orange juice
COCONUT BUTTER
125 g (4oz) butter
225 g (8oz) icing sugar, sifted
25 g (1oz) desiccated coconut
2 tablespoons orange juice

1 Preheat a moderately hot oven (190 deg C, 375 deg F, Gas 5), centre shelf. Grease a 20 cm by 30 cm (8in by 12in) Swiss roll tin and line with greased greaseproof paper.
2 Cream the butter and sugar until light and fluffy. Gradually beat in the eggs, a little at a time, beating well after each addition.
3 Add the orange rind, flour, coconut and orange juice and mix to a soft dropping consistency.
4 Transfer to the tin, spread out evenly. Bake 25-30 minutes, until firm to the touch. Turn out on to a wire rack, remove paper and allow to cool.
5 **To make the coconut butter:** Cream the butter until light and fluffy, then gradually beat in the icing sugar. Mix in the coconut and orange juice.
6 If necessary, trim the cake to make it level, then cut in half lengthways. Cut each piece into two layers. Sandwich the cake layers together with the coconut butter and spread a final layer on top. Transfer to a long plate.

GINGER CREAM ROLL

(Cuts into 5-6 slices)

2 eggs
50 g (2oz) castor sugar
50 g (2oz) self-raising flour
1 level teaspoon ground ginger
good pinch mixed spice
25 g (1oz) icing sugar
FILLING
1 tablespoon syrup from stem ginger jar
150 ml (5fl oz) double cream
50 g (2oz) stem ginger

1 Preheat a moderately hot oven (200 deg C, 400 deg F, Gas 6), centre shelf. Line a shallow Swiss-roll tin, 28 cm by 18 cm (11in by 7in), with greaseproof paper and grease lightly.
2 Whisk the eggs and sugar in a basin over a pan of hot water until the mixture is thick enough to hold the trail of the whisk when lifted. Lift off pan, whisk until cooled.
3 Sift in the flour and spices, fold in evenly. Pour into the tin, level the surface.
4 Bake for 8-10 minutes until risen and springy to touch and just drawing away from the edges.
5 Place greaseproof paper 2.5 cm (1in) larger than the tin on a board and sift on a little icing sugar. Turn the sponge on to this and gently peel off the lining paper. Trim the edges with a sharp knife if crisp and roll the sponge up lightly, enclosing the paper. Allow to cool on a wire rack.
6 **To make the filling:** Add the ginger syrup to the cream and whisk until stiff. Finely chop the ginger and fold into the cream. Unroll the sponge carefully, fill with cream and re-roll.
7 Sift the remaining icing sugar thickly on top.
8 Chill the cake before serving and take care to cut gently when slicing.

See picture opposite, below

POPPY SEED ROLL

(Cuts into 4-6 slices)

FILLING
100 g (4oz) dark poppy seeds
50 g (2oz) castor sugar
2 tablespoons milk
25 g (1oz) butter
PASTRY
100 g (4oz) plain flour
pinch of salt
25 g (1oz) cooking fat
25 g (1oz) margarine
about 6 tablespoons cold water to mix
GLAZING
a little beaten egg

1 **To make the filling:** Put all the ingredients into a small pan. Cook over low heat until the butter melts. Continue to cook very gently for a further 10 minutes, stirring. Leave on one side until quite cold.
2 Preheat a hot oven (220 deg C, 425 deg F, Gas 7), shelf just above centre. Lightly grease a baking sheet.
3 **To make the pastry:** Sift the flour and salt into a bowl. Rub in the fats finely. Mix to a stiff paste with water. Turn on to a floured surface and knead the pastry lightly until smooth.
4 Roll out into a rectangle measuring 27 cm by 22 cm (11in by 9in). Spread with filling to within 1.5 cm (½in) of the edges. Damp the edges with cold water then roll up like Swiss-roll, starting to roll from one of the longer sides.
5 Transfer to the baking sheet, brush the top with egg and bake about 25 minutes or until the pastry is crisp and golden brown.
6 Allow to cool on a wire rack and cut the roll into slices before serving.

Note: *If liked, the roll may be served warm as a dessert topped with softly whipped double cream.*

ROMANIAN-STYLE WALNUT SANDWICH

(Cuts into 8 slices)

175 g (6oz) butter, softened but not oily
175 g (6oz) castor sugar
1 teaspoon vanilla essence
3 eggs
175 g (6oz) self-raising flour
FILLING
100 g (4oz) walnuts
25 g (1oz) sugar
1 tablespoon rum
1 tablespoon milk
TOPPING
sifted icing sugar

1 Preheat a moderate oven (180 deg C, 350 deg F, Gas 4), centre shelf. Well grease two 20 cm (8in) sandwich tins, and line the bases with rounds of greased greaseproof paper.
2 In a large bowl, cream the butter, sugar and essence together until light and fluffy. Beat in whole eggs, one at a time, adding a tablespoon of flour with each.
3 With a large metal spoon, gently fold in the rest of the flour. Divide the mixture equally between the prepared tins. Bake for 25-30 minutes or until well risen and golden.
4 Cool in the tins 5 minutes, then transfer to a wire rack to finish cooling. Peel away the paper; leave until cold.
5 **To make the filling:** Finely grind the walnuts in a blender or coffee grinder then mix thoroughly with the rest of the ingredients. Sandwich the cake together with the walnut filling, then dust the top with icing sugar.

See picture opposite, above

Top: **Romanian-Style Walnut Sandwich,** *see opposite. Above:* **Ginger Cream Roll,** *see opposite.*

GINGER SPONGE

(Cuts into 6 slices)
125 g (4oz) self-raising flour
25 g (1oz) stem ginger in syrup, drained
3 large eggs
150 g (5oz) castor sugar
2 tablespoons stem ginger syrup
FILLING
75 ml (3fl oz) whipped double cream
ICING
100 g (4oz) icing sugar
1 tablespoon warm water
25 g (1oz) stem ginger in syrup, drained

1 Preheat a moderately hot oven (190 deg C, 375 deg F, Gas 5), shelf above centre. Line two 18 cm (7in) round sandwich tins with greaseproof paper, and brush lightly with oil.
2 Sift the flour twice.
3 Chop the stem ginger finely and mix with the flour.
4 Place eggs in a medium-sized deep bowl and stand over hot water. Whisk eggs to combine yolks and whites.
5 Gradually add the sugar, whisking well after each addition. Continue whisking until the mixture is thick enough to hold the trail of the whisk when it is lifted.
6 Remove the bowl from the water. Add a quarter of the flour and fold in with a metal spoon.
7 Gradually add the ginger syrup and remaining flour alternately, folding in carefully after each addition.
8 Turn into the prepared tins, smooth over the tops.
9 Bake for 15-20 minutes, or until the sponge springs back when lightly pressed with the fingertips.
10 Remove from the oven and leave in the tins for several minutes before turning out.
11 When cool, sandwich the two layers of sponge with whipped cream.
12 **To make the icing:** Sift the icing sugar into a small bowl and mix with warm water.
13 Spread the top of the cake with icing and decorate with thinly sliced stem ginger.

VICTORIA SANDWICH CAKE

(Makes one 18 cm/7in round sandwich cake)
125 g (4oz) butter or margarine
125 g (4oz) castor sugar
2 eggs, beaten
125 g (4oz) self-raising flour
pinch of salt
2 tablespoons jam, chocolate spread or butter icing
icing sugar for dredging

1 Preheat a moderately hot oven (190 deg C, 375 deg F, Gas 5), centre shelf. Grease two 18 cm (7in) round sandwich tins and line the bases with rounds of greased greaseproof paper.

2 Cream the butter with the sugar until light and fluffy. Gradually beat in the eggs, a little at a time, beating well after each addition.
3 Add the flour and salt and fold in evenly. If required, add a little water to the mixture, to make a soft dropping consistency.
4 Divide the mixture between the sandwich tins and level the surfaces.
5 Bake for about 25 minutes until firm to the touch and just beginning to shrink away from the sides of the tins.
6 Turn out on to a wire rack and remove the lining paper. Cool.
7 To serve, sandwich the cakes together with jam, chocolate spread or butter icing, and sprinkle the top with icing sugar.

VARIATIONS
Chocolate: Substitute 25 g (1oz) cocoa for the same quantity of flour.
Coffee: Add 2 teaspoons coffee essence in stage 3.
Orange or Lemon: Add the grated rind of one orange or lemon in stage 2.
Vanilla or Almond: Add 3-4 drops essence in stage 2.

BANANA SANDWICH CAKE

(Cuts into 8 slices)
100 g (4oz) butter or margarine
200 g (7oz) castor sugar
2 eggs, beaten
2 bananas, peeled and mashed
275 g (10oz) plain flour
1 level teaspoon baking powder
75 ml (3fl oz) water
1 level teaspoon bicarbonate of soda
FILLING
50 g (2oz) butter
100 g (4oz) icing sugar, sifted
grated rind ½ orange
4 teaspoons orange juice

1 Preheat a moderate oven (180 deg C, 350 deg F, Gas 4), shelf above centre. Grease two 20 cm (8in) sandwich tins and line them with either greased greaseproof paper or non-stick paper.
2 Cream the butter with the castor sugar until light and fluffy.
3 Gradually beat in the eggs a little at a time, beating well after each addition.
4 Stir in the mashed bananas. Sift the flour and baking powder and stir into the mixture.
5 Mix the water and bicarbonate of soda together and stir into the mixture. Divide the mixture evenly between the sandwich tins.
6 Bake for about ½ hour, until the centre springs back when pressed lightly with a finger.
7 Turn out on to a wire rack and remove the paper. Allow to cool.
8 **To make the filling:** Cream the butter till light and fluffy, beat in icing sugar, stir in orange rind and juice.
9 Sandwich the cooled cake layers with the filling.

20

FEATHERED CITRUS CAKE

(Cuts into about 10 slices)
175 g (6oz) butter or margarine
175 g (6oz) castor sugar
3 eggs
finely grated rind 1 orange
finely gated rind ½ lemon
175 g (6oz) self-raising flour
40 g (1½oz) desiccated coconut
BUTTER AND GLACE ICING
75 g (3oz) butter
250 g (9oz) icing sugar, sifted
75 g (3oz) marmalade
juice ½ orange
orange food colouring

1 Preheat a moderately hot oven (190 deg C, 375 deg F, Gas 5), centre shelf. Lightly grease two 19-20 cm (7½-8in) sandwich tins and line the bases with greased greaseproof paper.
2 Cream the butter and sugar until soft and light, beat in the eggs one at a time with the grated rinds. Sift and fold in flour evenly. Divide between tins, level the surfaces.
3 Cook for 25 minutes, unti just firm when pressed with fingers. Loosen edges, turn out gently on to a wire rack.
4 Toast the coconut until light brown. Allow to cool.
5 **To make the butter icing:** Cream the butter, then gradually add 150 g (5oz) icing sugar. Beat in the marmalade. Sandwich the cake with some of this.
6 **To make the glacé icing:** Mix the remaining sugar with enough orange juice to give a thick icing. Spread over the top of the cake, keeping a spoonful back. Colour this strongly with orange colouring and pipe parallel lines at 2.5 cm (1in) intervals across the cake. Immediately drag the tip of a knife first one way, then the other, across the cake at right angles to the piping, to give a feathered effect. Leave to set.
7 Spread the remaining butter icing round the edge of the cake and press on coconut to coat it.

MOIST CINNAMON CAKE

(Makes one 23 cm/9in square cake)
125 g (4oz) butter or margarine
50 g (2oz) soft brown sugar
50 g (2oz) black treacle
175 g (6oz) golden syrup
225 g (8oz) plain flour
2 level tablespoons ground cinnamon
1 level teaspoon bicarbonate of soda
150 ml (5fl oz) milk
2 eggs

1 Preheat a warm oven (170 deg C, 325 deg F, Gas 3), shelf above centre. Grease a 23 cm (9in) square cake tin

and then line it with greased greaseproof paper.
2 Place the butter, sugar, treacle and golden syrup in a saucepan and heat gently, stirring, until the sugar has dissolved.
3 Sift the flour, cinnamon and bicarbonate of soda into a mixing bowl, make a well in the centre.
4 Add the syrup mixture, stir well, adding the milk to make a smooth batter. Lightly whisk the eggs and stir in. Transfer the mixture to the prepared tin.
5 Bake for 50-60 minutes until the surface springs back when lightly pressed with the fingertips. Cool for 5 minutes in the tin. Turn on to a wire rack, remove the paper and leave to cool completely.
6 Keep for at least 24 hours before serving. Store in an airtight container.

MADEIRA CAKE

(Makes one 20 cm/8in round cake)
225 g (8oz) butter
275 g (10oz) castor sugar
grated rind 1 lemon
5 eggs
375 g (13oz) plain flour
2 level teaspoons baking powder
pinch of salt
50 ml (2fl oz) milk
a thin slice citron peel

1 Preheat a moderate oven (180 deg C, 350 deg F, Gas 4), centre shelf. Grease a 20 cm (8in) deep round cake tin and line with greased greaseproof paper.
2 Cream the butter, sugar and lemon rind until light and fluffy. Beat in the eggs, one at a time, adding a little of the flour with each.
3 Sift in remaining flour, baking powder and salt and fold into the mixture with the milk. Turn into the prepared tin and level the surface.
4 Bake for ½ hour and then place the slice of citron peel on top. Continue baking for a further 1-1½ hours until a skewer inserted in the centre comes out clean.
5 Cool in the tin for 15 minutes, then turn on to a wire rack, remove paper and leave to cool completely.

chapter 3
Chocolate and Coffee Cakes

These are among the favourite flavours, so they have a chapter to themselves. Here are some cakes simple enough for everyday, and some so rich and festive they can be served at the most special occasion

CHOCOLATE AND ORANGE CAKE

(Makes one 18 cm/7in round cake)
225 g (8oz) plain flour
1 level teaspoon baking powder
175 g (6oz) butter, softened but not oily
175 g (6oz) castor sugar
grated rind 1 medium-sized orange
3 eggs
2 milk flake bars, crushed
4 tablespoons milk
ORANGE BUTTER ICING
100 g (4oz) butter, softened
225 g (8oz) icing sugar, sifted
juice ½ orange
TOPPING
1 orange, cut in segments
a little crushed milk flake bar

1 Preheat a warm oven (170 deg C, 325 deg F, Gas 3), centre shelf. Well-grease the base and sides of a deep 18 cm (7in) round cake tin. Line with greased greaseproof paper.
2 Sift the flour and baking powder on to a plate. Cream the butter, sugar and orange rind together until light, fluffy and very pale in colour. Beat in whole eggs, one at a time, adding a tablespoon of the flour with each.
3 Stir in the crushed chocolate then, with a large metal spoon, fold in the flour alternately with milk.
4 Transfer to prepared tin, smooth top with a knife. Bake for about 1½ hours until well risen and golden.
5 Leave in the tin 10 minutes then turn out on to a wire rack and carefully peel away the lining paper.
6 **To make the butter icing:** Beat the butter, sugar and

orange juice together until light and fluffy. Refrigerate about ½ hour or until the cream firms up.
7 When the cake is completely cold, slice it in half horizontally and fill with just under half the butter icing. Swirl the rest of the icing over the top. Arrange orange segments in the centre and spoon crushed flake bar around the edge.
See picture opposite

CHOCOLATE CREAM CAKE

(Makes one 20 cm/8in shallow cake)
125 g (4oz) digestive biscuits
75 g (3oz) butter or margarine
2 tablespoons golden syrup
2 teaspoons cocoa
4 teaspoons boiling water
25 g (1oz) castor sugar
75 g (3oz) self-raising flour
1 large egg plus 1 egg yolk
142 ml (5fl oz) carton soured cream
8-12 chocolate buttons

1 Preheat a moderate oven (180 deg C, 350 deg F, Gas 4), shelf above centre. Grease a 20 cm (8in) flan ring and a baking sheet.
2 Place the biscuits in a plastic bag and crush with a rolling pin. Melt 25 g (1oz) of the butter and one tablespoon of the syrup, add the crushed biscuits. Spread in the base of the prepared flan ring.
3 Blend the cocoa and boiling water, allow to cool.
4 Cream together the remaining butter and the sugar until light and fluffy. Add the remaining tablespoon of golden syrup and beat well.
5 Add one tablespoon of the weighed flour and the

*It is important to follow **either** the metric **or** the imperial weights and measures in any one recipe*

Chocolate and Orange Cake, *see opposite*

whole egg and beat well. Add the blended cocoa and one tablespoon of the soured cream and beat well.

6 Fold in the remainder of the flour. Spread the mixture on the biscuit crumb base.

7 Cook for 20-25 minutes, or until the centre of the sponge is firm when pressed lightly with the fingertips.

8 Beat the remaining egg yolk and soured cream together. Spread on the cooked cake and decorate with chocolate buttons. Return to the oven for 5 minutes until the soured cream has set.

9 Remove the cake from the oven and leave until cold.

10 Carefully remove from flan ring, place on a dish.

CHOCOLATE EASTER CAKE

(Cuts into 12 slices)

175 g (6oz) butter
75 g (3oz) castor sugar
75 g (3oz) soft dark brown sugar
2 level teaspoons black treacle
3 eggs, beaten
175 g (6oz) self-raising flour
2 level tablespoons cocoa
about 225 g (8oz) apricot jam, warmed
75 g (3oz) butter
175 g (6oz) icing sugar, sifted
1 tablespoon hot water
50 g (2oz) plain chocolate
226 g (8oz) packet almond paste
halved almonds

1 Preheat a moderate oven (180 deg C, 350 deg F, Gas 4), centre shelf. Grease two 19 cm (7½in) sandwich tins and line the bases with greased greaseproof paper.

2 Cream the butter, sugars and treacle together until light and fluffy. Beat in the eggs gradually. Sift the flour with the cocoa, fold into creamed mixture, add a little water, if needed, to make a soft dropping consistency.

3 Divide the mixture between the tins and smooth the surfaces. Bake for 25-30 minutes until springy to touch. Turn on to a wire rack, remove lining papers and cool.

4 Cut each cake in half horizontally, spread with most of the jam, sandwich together again.

5 Cream the butter, then gradually beat in the icing sugar and one tablespoon hot water. Melt the chocolate in a basin over hot water, beat into the icing. Sandwich the two cakes together with half the chocolate icing.

6 Roll out the almond paste into a long strip to fit round the sides of the cake. (Use a little icing sugar if inclined to stick during rolling.) Brush the sides of the cake with the remaining jam, fit and press on the almond paste, joining the edges neatly.

7 Spread the remaining icing on top of the cake, make a pattern of radiating 'spokes' marking them in with flat of knife from centre to edge and meeting neatly with the almond paste. Decorate with toasted halved almonds.

CHOCOLATE YOGURT CAKE

(Makes one 20 cm/8in cake)

150 g (5oz) plain flour
25 g (1oz) cocoa
½ level teaspoon bicarbonate of soda
½ level teaspoon salt
50 g (2oz) butter
300 g (11oz) castor sugar
2 eggs, beaten
150 ml (5fl oz) natural yogurt
LEMON FILLING
50 g (2oz) butter
100 g (4oz) icing sugar, sifted
1 teaspoon lemon juice
1 tablespoon yogurt or milk

1 Preheat a moderate oven (180 deg C, 350 deg F, Gas 4), centre shelf. Grease two 20 cm (8in) sandwich tins and line the bases with greased greaseproof paper.

2 Sift the flour, cocoa, bicarbonate of soda and salt.

3 Cream the butter in a mixing bowl until light and fluffy. Then using an electric whisk or rotary beater mix in the sugar and eggs. When well blended, gradually beat in the yogurt to make a smooth batter.

4 Fold in the sifted mixture until well blended. Divide between the tins and spread out evenly.

5 Bake for 35-40 minutes until firm to the touch. Turn out on to a wire rack, remove paper and allow to cool.

6 **To make the lemon filling:** Cream the butter until light and fluffy, then gradually beat in the icing sugar and lemon juice. Mix in the yogurt or milk.

7 Sandwich the cakes together with the filling and, if liked, sprinkle the top of the cake with a little icing sugar. This is a moist cake which keeps well for up to a week.

CHOCOLATE DESSERT CAKE

(Makes one 19 cm/7½in round cake)

75 g (3oz) plain chocolate
15 g (½oz) margarine
3 eggs
125 g (4oz) icing sugar, sifted
a few drops vanilla essence
75 g (3oz) plain flour
½ level teaspoon baking powder
FILLING
½ orange flavoured jelly
150 ml (5fl oz) boiling water
250 ml (10fl oz) double or whipping cream

1 Preheat a moderate oven (180 deg C, 350 deg F, Gas 4), centre shelf. Lightly oil a 19 cm (7½in) round cake tin, and line the base with greased greaseproof paper.

2 Break 50 g (2oz) of the chocolate into pieces, put into a basin with the margarine, and heat together over boiling water until melted. Stir to blend.

3 Meanwhile, separate the yolks from the whites of the eggs. Put the yolks in a bowl, add the icing sugar, and

whisk together until thick. Add the vanilla essence.

4 Sift together the flour and baking powder and, using a metal spoon, stir carefully into the whisked yolks with the melted chocolate.

5 Whisk egg whites until stiff, fold gently into mixture.

6 Turn into prepared tin, spread evenly, bake ½ hour until springy to touch. Cool on wire rack. Remove paper.

7 **To make the filling:** Meanwhile, completely dissolve the jelly in boiling water, leave to cool until nearly set.

8 Whisk 200 ml (7fl oz) of the cream until softly stiff, and stir in the nearly set jelly. Leave to set.

9 Cut the cake in half horizontally. Stir the jelly cream with a fork, spread on one half of the cake and cover with the other half.

10 Whisk the remaining cream and spread over the top.

11 Grate the remaining chocolate coarsely, and sprinkle all over the cream to decorate.

12 Keep the cake in the refrigerator or a cool larder until ready to serve.

CHOCOLATE ALMOND TORTE

(Cuts into about 8 slices)

2 egg whites
100 g (4oz) castor sugar
50 g (2oz) ground almonds
50 g (2oz) fresh white breadcrumbs
¼ teaspoon almond essence
CHOCOLATE FILLING
50 g (2oz) sugar
3 level teaspoons cocoa
150 ml (5fl oz) milk
2 egg yolks
175 g (6oz) butter
DECORATION
15 g (½oz) flaked almonds, toasted

1 Preheat a warm oven (170 deg C, 325 deg F, Gas 3), shelves above and below centre. Line two baking sheets with greaseproof paper, mark an 18 cm (7in) circle on each and brush with oil.

2 Whisk the egg whites until stiff. Then whisk in half the sugar. Mix together the remaining sugar, ground almonds and breadcrumbs; using a metal spoon, fold into the meringue. Fold in the almond essence.

3 Divide the mixture in half and spread on the baking sheets on the two marked circles.

4 Bake for about 20 minutes, until golden. Cool on a wire rack, carefully removing the paper when cool.

5 **To make the chocolate filling:** Place the sugar, cocoa and milk in a saucepan and heat gently, stirring, until sugar and cocoa dissolve, then bring to the boil. Beat the yolks until creamy, then pour in the milk mixture. Stir well, return to the pan and heat. Cook over a medium heat until the mixture coats the back of a wooden spoon; do not boil. Cover with cling film and leave until cold.

6 Beat the butter until creamy. Then gradually whisk the butter into the custard, whisking well.

7 Sandwich the almond rounds together with slightly less than half the chocolate filling. Spread the remainder on top and sides. Press flaked almonds around the sides.

MOCHA RING

(Cuts into 12 slices)

225 g (8oz) butter or margarine
175 g (6oz) castor sugar
4 eggs
200 g (7oz) self-raising flour
50 g (2oz) cocoa
BUTTER ICING
2 heaped teaspoons instant coffee powder
2-3 tablespoons very hot water
125 g (4oz) butter, softened
175 g (6oz) icing sugar, sifted
1 rounded tablespoon cocoa, sifted
GLACE ICING
225 g (8oz) icing sugar, sifted
1 heaped teaspoon instant coffee powder

1 Preheat a warm oven (170 deg C, 325 deg F, Gas 3), centre shelf. Grease a 1¾-litre (3-pint) ring tin.

2 Cream the butter and sugar until soft. Beat in the eggs one at a time, beating well after each addition. Sift on the flour and cocoa and fold in.

3 Spoon into the tin and level the surface. Bake for 50 60 minutes, until just firm when pressed. Turn out carefully on to a wire rack.

4 **To make the butter icing:** Dissolve the coffee in 2 tablespoons very hot water and stir into the butter and icing sugar. Beat until smooth, adding a little extra water if necessary.

5 Slice the cake in half horizontally and sandwich with some butter icing. Beat the cocoa into the rest of the icing.

6 **To make the glacé icing:** Blend the icing sugar with the instant coffee dissolved in one teaspoon hot water. Add extra water to make a smooth icing and spread over the cake to cover completely. Leave until set.

7 Pipe remaining butter icing over the cake, using a fine writing pipe, to give a lattice or zigzag pattern.

8 Place the cake on a serving plate. Using a small star tube, pipe remaining chocolate butter icing round base.

COFFEE LAYER CAKE

(Cuts into 12 slices)
125 g (4oz) butter
125 g (4oz) chocolate drops for cooking
4 eggs
½ level teaspoon salt
175 g (6oz) castor sugar
125 g (4oz) plain flour
25 g (1oz) chopped walnuts
BUTTER ICING
125 g (4oz) butter
250 g (8oz) icing sugar, sifted
2 level teaspoons instant coffee powder dissolved in 1
   teaspoon boiling water
25 g (1oz) chopped walnuts
25 g (1oz) walnuts, for decoration

1 Put the butter and chocolate in a bowl over a pan of hot water. Stir until melted. Remove from heat and cool.
2 Preheat a moderate oven (180 deg C, 350 deg F, Gas 4), shelves above and below centre. Grease three 16-18 cm (6½-7in) sandwich tins and line the bases with non-stick paper.
3 Put the eggs, salt and sugar in a mixing bowl over a pan of hot water and whisk until light in colour and thick; the whisk should leave a trail when lifted.
4 Add the cooled chocolate mixture, flour and chopped walnuts and fold in gently with a large metal spoon.
5 Divide the mixture between the tins. Bake for 20-25 minutes until cooked. Cool in the tins for a minute, loosen edges, turn on wire rack to cool. Remove paper.
6 To make the butter icing: Cream the butter then gradually beat in all the icing sugar and the dissolved coffee. Put one third of the icing into another bowl. Mix the chopped walnuts into the larger amount.
7 To decorate the cake: Sandwich the 3 sponge rounds together with the walnut icing. Spread and swirl coffee icing on top and decorate with walnuts.
See picture opposite and on the cover

COFFEE CARAMEL GATEAU

(Cuts into 8 portions)
3 eggs
75 g (3oz) castor sugar
75 g (3oz) plain flour
⅛ level teaspoon baking powder
COFFEE BUTTER ICING
1 level tablespoon instant coffee powder
a little boiling water
125 g (4oz) butter or margarine
225 g (8oz) icing sugar, sifted
CARAMEL
50 g (2oz) castor sugar
2 tablespoons water

1 Preheat a moderately hot oven (190 deg C, 375 deg F, Gas 5), centre shelf. Grease two 19 cm (7½in) sandwich

tins, line the bases with greased greaseproof paper.
2 Whisk the eggs and sugar in a mixing bowl over hot water until pale and thick enough to support a trail, falling from the lifted whisk, for a few seconds. Remove from over water and continue whisking until the bowl is nearly cold.
3 Sift the flour and baking powder together. Sift half into whisked mixture, fold in lightly with a large metal spoon. Repeat with the remaining flour until evenly mixed. Divide between the tins, shake or tap to spread evenly.
4 Bake for about 20 minutes until risen and brown. Loosen the edges from the tin, turn on to a wire rack and remove the papers. Cool.
5 To make the butter icing: Dissolve the coffee in one tablespoon boiling water. Cream the butter until light and fluffy then gradually beat in the icing sugar and coffee. Beat until smooth adding another teaspoon hot water if necessary.
6 Sandwich the cakes together with some icing. Spread more icing over the top and sides to coat completely. Place on a serving plate. Use a small star tube to pipe round the top edge. Pipe 4 'spokes' across the top to divide the cake into 8 sections or mark the cake with a knife and mark a pattern round the edge with a fork.
7 To make the caramel: Place a piece of lightly oiled greaseproof paper on a baking sheet. In a small pan heat the sugar with 2 tablespoons water over low heat. When dissolved, boil and cook rapidly until rich golden brown, pour immediately on to oiled paper. Leave to cool.
8 Turn the paper and caramel upside down on a baking sheet. Tap firmly with a rolling pin to crush the caramel into quite small pieces. Spoon into 4 sections between stars or lines on top of cake, press remainder round the side of the cake.

Coffee Layer Cake, *see opposite*

27

chapter 4
Special Cakes and Gâteaux

The beautiful, tempting cakes you can serve at
almost any meal. For summer, there are lovely gâteaux
to top and fill with fresh strawberries,
raspberries, redcurrants and cream; others are made
with oranges, lemons, nuts . . .

GATEAU MARGOT

(Serves 8-12)
FILLING
1 envelope gelatine
juice ½ lemon
4 tablespoons water
250 ml (½ pint) double cream
75 g (3oz) icing sugar
250 ml (½ pint) unsweetened strawberry purée made
   from 350 g (12oz) strawberries
SPONGE CAKE
4 eggs
125 g (4oz) castor sugar
125 g (4oz) plain flour
⅛ level teaspoon salt
whole strawberries to decorate

1 Preheat a moderately hot oven (190 deg C, 375 deg F,
Gas 5), centre shelf. Grease two 20 cm (8in) sandwich tins
and line the bases with greased greaseproof paper.
2 To make the filling: Place the gelatine in a small
saucepan, stir in the lemon juice and the water. Leave to
soak for a few minutes, then heat slowly until all the
gelatine has melted.
3 Whisk the cream and icing sugar until thick.
4 Combine the gelatine with the strawberry purée and
make it up to 550 ml (1 pint) with cold water, mix it into
the cream and leave aside in a cold place to set while the
cake is being made.
5 To make the sponge cake: Separate the eggs and whisk
the whites until very stiff.
6 Whisk the yolks and sugar together until thick, fluffy
and much paler in colour, add the whisked whites and

continue whisking until the mixture is well blended.
7 Sift the flour and salt together and carefully fold into
the egg mixture; when evenly mixed, divide the mixture
between the sandwich tins. Bake the cake for about 20
minutes until well risen, golden brown and firm to touch.
Turn out on to a wire rack and leave to cool.
8 Cut each cake in half, use about half the strawberry
jelly cream to sandwich the layers of cake together, and
use the remainder to completely cover the cake, smoo-
thing it off finally with a hot palette knife.
9 Decorate the cake with whole strawberries, chill in a
refrigerator. Serve as a cake or a dessert.

STRAWBERRY CARAMEL RING

(Serves 6)
CHOUX PASTRY
65 g (2½oz) plain flour
pinch of salt
150 ml (5fl oz) water
50 g (2oz) butter or margarine
2 eggs
FILLING
150 ml (5fl oz) double cream
50 g (2oz) castor sugar
225 g (8oz) strawberries, hulled
CARAMEL
50 g (2oz) castor sugar
2 tablespoons water

1 Preheat a moderately hot oven (200 deg C, 400 deg F,
Gas 6), shelf above centre. Grease a baking sheet and
mark a circle, using a 15 cm (6in) saucer as a guide.
2 Sift the flour and salt on to a plate.
3 Place the water in a saucepan and add the butter. Heat

*It is important to follow **either** the metric **or** the imperial weights
and measures in any one recipe*

gently until the fat has melted, then bring to the boil, remove from the heat and quickly add the flour all at once. Beat until smooth. Cool for 5 minutes.

4 Lightly whisk the eggs, then beat gradually into the cooled mixture, beating well after each addition, to make a smooth, shiny paste.

5 Spread spoonfuls of the mixture evenly on the baking sheet within the marked circle, leaving a hole in the centre of about 5 cm (2in).

6 Bake for ½ hour, then reduce oven temperature to moderate (180 deg C, 350 deg F, Gas 4) and remove the ring from the oven. Cut a few slits round the ring, then return to the oven for 10 minutes until crisp. Cool on a wire rack.

7 To make the filling: Whip the cream until just stiff and then fold in the sugar.

8 Cut the ring horizontally in half and lift off the top carefully. Place the lower half on a serving plate. Fill with most of the cream. Arrange the strawberries on top and spread with remaining cream. Cover with the ring top. Chill while making the caramel.

9 To make the caramel: Place the sugar and the water in a small saucepan, heat gently until the sugar has dissolved, shaking the pan round occasionally. Bring to the boil and boil until the sugar syrup turns rich caramel brown.

10 Pour immediately over the top of the choux ring, allowing it to trickle down the sides. Leave to set.

Note: *This cake is best made the day it is required.*

RASPBERRY LAYER CAKE

(Serves 8)

125 g (4oz) butter or margarine
125 g (4oz) castor sugar
2 eggs
125 g (4oz) self-raising flour, sifted
FILLING
250 ml (½ pint) milk
1 vanilla pod
1 egg
1 egg yolk
50 g (2oz) castor sugar
25 g (1oz) plain flour
DECORATION
450 g (1lb) fresh raspberries
150 ml (5fl oz) double cream
icing sugar for sprinkling

1 Preheat a moderately hot oven (190 deg C, 375 deg F, Gas 5), centre shelf. Lightly oil two 18 cm (7in) sandwich tins, lightly coat with flour.

2 Cream the butter and sugar together until light and creamy.

3 Beat eggs, gradually add to the mixture, fold in flour.

4 Divide the mixture between the tins. Level the surfaces. Cook for 20-25 minutes until the top springs back when gently pressed with the fingertips.

5 Remove from tins, allow to cool on a wire rack.

6 To make the filling: Place the milk and vanilla pod in a pan, bring gently to the boil. Remove pan from heat.

7 Place the egg, egg yolk, sugar and flour in a bowl and

beat well. Remove the vanilla pod from milk, gradually stir the milk into the creamed mixture. Return to the pan and bring to the boil, stirring; simmer for 2 minutes. Remove and allow to cool.

8 To assemble: Cut each sponge cake in half through the centre to give 4 rounds.

9 Pick over the raspberries, reserving a quarter of the best berries for the top. Lightly mash the remainder.

10 Spread the base sponge with some of the crushed raspberries and some of the filling, cover with a sponge layer, repeat until all the fillings are used up, leaving the top sponge plain.

11 Whisk the cream until softly stiff, spread over the top.

12 Arrange remaining raspberries over the top and sprinkle with icing sugar.

STRAWBERRY CREAM MERINGUE GATEAU

(Serves 6-8)

150 g (5oz) plain flour
25 g (1oz) cornflour
2 level teaspoons baking powder
½ level teaspoon salt
150 g (5oz) castor sugar
100 ml (3½fl oz) corn oil
100 ml (3½fl oz) water
2 eggs
MERINGUE
1 egg white
40 g (1½oz) castor sugar
15 g (½oz) icing sugar
DECORATION
350 g (12oz) strawberries
250 ml (½ pint) double cream

1 Preheat a moderately hot oven (190 deg C, 375 deg F, Gas 5), towards top and centre shelf. Line the bases of two 18 cm (7in) sandwich tins. Lightly brush with oil.

2 Sift the dry ingredients into a large mixing bowl.

3 Mix the oil and water together in a separate bowl.

4 Separate the egg yolks and whites, and add the yolks to the oil and water. Mix lightly with a fork.

5 Stir into the dry ingredients to make a smooth slack batter. Whisk egg whites stiffly, fold into the batter.

6 Divide into the prepared tins and bake for 25-30 minutes. Remove from oven and cool on a wire rack. Switch off oven.

7 To make the meringue: Place the egg white in a clean bowl, whisk until stiff and dry. Sift the castor and icing sugar and whisk a spoonful at a time into the egg white.

8 Place the meringue into a piping bag fitted with a fluted vegetable nozzle. Pipe about 12-18 small rosettes of meringue on to a piece of waxed paper on a baking sheet.

9 Place the meringues in the coolest possible oven, and leave to dry out for about 2 hours. If the oven is too hot, leave the door open.

10 When cool, store in airtight container until wanted.

11 To decorate: Hull the strawberries and reserve 12-18 of the best berries. Lightly mash the rest.

12 Whisk the cream until softly stiff and fold in the

mashed strawberries. Sandwich the sponges together with just under half this mixture. Spread remainder on the top of the cake and arrange the whole berries and meringues alternately over it.

See picture opposite, above

STRAWBERRY CHOUX GATEAU

(Serves 8)

PASTRY BASE
25 g (1oz) lard or cooking fat
40 g (1½oz) butter or margarine
150 g (5oz) plain flour
CHOUX PASTRY
65 g (2½oz) plain flour
pinch of salt
50 g (2oz) butter or margarine
150 ml (5fl oz) water
2 eggs
CUSTARD CREAM
25 g (1oz) plain flour
50 g (2oz) castor sugar
1 egg, lightly beaten
275 ml (½ pint) milk
½ teaspoon vanilla essence
DECORATION
275 ml (½ pint) fresh double cream
2 tablespoons strawberry jam
50 g (2oz) plain dessert chocolate
450 g (1lb) strawberries, hulled

To make the pastry base: Rub lard or cooking fat and butter or margarine into the plain flour until the mixture looks like breadcrumbs. Stir in 5 teaspoons cold water to make a stiff dough. Draw the mixture together and knead it lightly.

2 Roll the pastry out, cut into a round about 25 cm (10in) in diameter, slip it on to a baking sheet and prick well with a fork. Chill while making the choux pastry.

3 Preheat a moderately hot oven (200 deg C, 400 deg F, Gas 6), shelf above centre.

4 To make the choux pastry: Sift the flour and salt on to a piece of greaseproof paper. Gently heat the water with the butter. When the fat has melted, bring to the boil. Remove from heat and immediately add all the flour. Beat until smooth. Cool for 5 minutes.

5 Lightly whisk the eggs, then beat gradually into the cooled mixture, beating well after each addition to make a smooth, shiny paste.

6 Brush the edge of the pastry base with a little cold water. Spoon or pipe the choux pastry with a 1.5 cm (½in) plain nozzle along the edge of the pastry to form a ring.

7 Bake for 10 minutes. If pastry is ballooning in centre, prick with a fork. Now increase the oven heat to hot (220 deg C, 425 deg F, Gas 7) and cook for a further 20 minutes or until the pastry and choux are cooked. If the pastry appears to be browning too much, cover with foil. Remove from oven. Pierce choux ring in several places, so steam can escape. Allow to cool.

8 To make the custard cream: Stir the flour and sugar into the lightly beaten egg. Heat the milk almost to boiling point, stir about 3 tablespoons of it into the egg and flour. When smoothly blended mix in remaining milk.

9 Return the cream to the saucepan, add the vanilla essence and stir over a gentle heat until it thickens; place aside until cold.

10 To assemble the gâteau: Split the choux ring in half horizontally, lift off the top half and place aside.

11 Spread the cooled custard cream on the pastry base in the centre of the ring.

12 Stiffly whip the cream and pipe or spread into the bottom layer of choux.

13 Heat the jam with one tablespoon of water to thin it, allow to cool.

14 Measure 2 teaspoons of water into a bowl, break in the chocolate and stand the bowl over a pan of hot water until the chocolate has melted. Carefully spoon it over the top layer of the choux.

15 Spoon the jam over the whipped cream then cover with the top layer of choux.

16 Fill the centre of the ring with strawberries. Serve as soon as possible.

REDCURRANT AND ORANGE DESSERT CAKE

(Serves 8)

175 g (6oz) butter or margarine
175 g (6oz) castor sugar
a few drops vanilla essence
3 eggs, lightly beaten
175 g (6oz) self-raising flour
2 tablespoons warm water
225-350 g (8-12oz) frozen redcurrants, almost thawed
4-6 level tablespoons castor sugar
2-3 oranges
275 ml (½ pint) double cream

1 Preheat a moderate oven (180 deg C, 350 deg F, Gas 4), centre shelf. Grease two 20 cm (8in) sandwich tins and line the bases with greased greaseproof paper.

2 Cream the butter, sugar and vanilla essence until light and fluffy. Beat in the egg a little at a time, beating after each addition.

3 Sift the flour, fold into the creamed mixture with the warm water. Turn the mixture into the tins and level the surfaces.

4 Bake for 30-35 minutes until cooked. When lightly pressed with a finger, the mixture should spring back.

5 Turn out, remove paper, allow to cool on a wire rack.

6 Mix the almost thawed redcurrants with 3-5 tablespoons of castor sugar according to taste.

7 Cut away the peel and pith from the oranges and cut oranges into neat segments – add any orange juice to the redcurrants. Select neat segments of orange and reserve for decoration, keep remainder for filling.

8 Whisk the cream with one tablespoon castor sugar until thick enough to stand in peaks.

9 Spread half the cream on one cake round. Top with almost half the redcurrant mixture and orange segments reserved for filling.

10 Put the second cake round on top and press down

Top: **Strawberry Cream Meringue Gâteau,** *see page 29; Above:* **Redcurrant and Orange Dessert Cake,** *see opposite*

lightly. Spread remaining cream over the surface, spoon remaining redcurrants on top and decorate with orange reserved for decoration.

11 Chill until required.

Note: *Raspberries may be used instead of redcurrants.*
See picture on page 31, below

BLACKCURRANT GATEAU

(Serves 6-8)
SPONGE CAKE
4 eggs
100g (4oz) castor sugar
100g (4oz) plain flour
75 g (3oz) unsalted butter, melted and cooled
FILLING
450 g (1lb) blackcurrants, prepared
125 g (4oz) granulated sugar
DECORATION
250 ml (½ pint) double cream
2 level tablespoons castor sugar
25 g (1oz) plain chocolate, grated

1 **To make the sponge cake:** Preheat a moderately hot oven (190 deg C, 375 deg F, Gas 5), centre shelf.
2 Grease a 20 cm (8in) round cake tin, and line the base with a round of greased greaseproof paper.
3 Put the eggs and castor sugar into a mixing bowl over a pan of hot, but not boiling water. Whisk together until thick and creamy and until the mixture will hold the whisk's trail for 5 seconds. Remove bowl from pan.
4 Sift the flour gently over the surface of the whisked mixture, fold in carefully with a metal spoon. Very carefully fold in the cooled butter, a little at a time.
5 Pour into the prepared tin. Bake for 25-30 minutes until well risen and firm to touch. Cool on a wire rack.
6 **To make the filling:** Put the blackcurrants in a pan with the granulated sugar, cover and cook gently for about 20 minutes until soft. Taste for sweetness, and adjust if necessary. Allow the mixture to cool.
7 Slice the cooled sponge cake into three layers. Place the bottom layer on a cake board, spread with half the balckcurrants, including juice. Place the centre layer of sponge on the blackcurrants, spread with rest of black currants and juice, top with remaining sponge layer. Press the layers lightly together.
8 **To decorate:** Whip the cream and castor sugar together until just thick enough to hold a shape. Spread over the cake to cover completely. Mark the cream with a knife into swirls. Sprinkle the top with grated chocolate.

APRICOT CHEESECAKE

(Serves 6)
BISCUIT CRUMB BASE
8 small digestive biscuits
50 g (2oz) butter
FILLING
1 large egg
50 g (2oz) castor sugar
225 g (8oz) curd cheese
225 g (8oz) cream cheese
grated rind and juice 1 lemon
½ teaspoon vanilla essence
1 level teaspoon cornflour
25 g (1oz) sultanas
TOPPING
400 g (14oz) can apricot fruit filling
175 ml (6fl oz) double cream
15 g (½oz) flaked almonds

1 Preheat a moderate oven (180 deg C, 350 deg F, Gas 4), centre shelf. Well-grease a round 20 cm (8in) loose-based cake tin.
2 Place the digestive biscuits in a bowl or large paper bag and crush with a rolling pin until quite fine.
3 Melt the butter in a pan.
4 Stir in the biscuit crumbs so that all the butter is absorbed and the crumbs are coated.
5 Turn the crumb mixture into the tin and, using the back of a spoon, press firmly on to the base.
6 **To make the filling:** Place the egg and sugar in a bowl and beat well to mix.
7 Add the curd and cream cheeses, lemon rind and juice and mix well.
8 Add the vanilla essence, cornflour and sultanas and mix thoroughly.
9 Turn the filling on to the crumb base in the tin and smooth the surface.
10 Bake for ½ hour until the filling is set. Turn off the heat and leave in the oven for a further ½ hour to cool (this prevents the cheesecake from sinking). Remove from oven and leave until cold.
11 Remove the cheesecake from the tin by standing the base on an upturned jam jar and carefully loosening the sides. Carefully remove the cake from the base, using a fish slice and a palette knife, then place it on a round serving dish.
12 **To make the topping:** Spread three-quarters of the can of filling over the top of the cheesecake, arranging the apricot pieces evenly (the remainder makes a good ice-cream sauce).
13 Place the cream in a bowl and whisk until it just holds its shape. Place the whisked cream in a large piping bag fitted with a star nozzle. Pipe cream rosettes around edge of cake. Sprinkle the cream with the flaked almonds. Serve chilled.

Note: *The cheesecake can be made the day before it is required, and decorated shortly before serving.*

APRICOT GATEAU

(Serves 8-10)

75 g (3oz) granulated sugar
275 ml (½ pint) water
450 g (1lb) apricots
3 large eggs
75 g (3oz) castor sugar
75 g (3oz) plain flour
½ level teaspoon baking powder
pinch of salt
100 g (4oz) shelled hazelnuts
2-3 tablespoons brandy
425 ml (¾ pint) fresh double cream
150 ml (5fl oz) fresh single cream
1 level tablespoon icing sugar
½ teaspoon vanilla essence
extra sugar

1 Put the granulated sugar and water into a saucepan, heat slowly until the sugar has dissolved. Boil the syrup rapidly for 2 minutes.
2 Wash the apricots, cut through the flesh round the stone of each, and remove the stones (if obstinate, remove when fruit is cooked).
3 Add the apricots to the syrup, bring to the boil and cook gently for about 15 minutes or until tender. Allow to cool.
4 Preheat a moderately hot oven (190 deg C, 375 deg F, Gas 5), shelf above centre. Grease a 23 cm (9in) sandwich tin and line the base with greased greaseproof paper.
5 Select a saucepan that a mixing bowl will rest neatly and securely over. Half fill pan with water, bring to the boil, then place the pan on a heat protected surface.
6 Break the eggs into a bowl and add the castor sugar. Put the bowl on the saucepan then whisk, with a rotary beater, until the mixture is thick and foamy (this will take about 15 minutes), or until a trail is left in the mixture when the whisk is lifted.
7 Remove bowl from pan and continue whisking until the mixture is cold.
Note: If using an electric hand mixer, the heat is not necessary.
8 Sift the flour, baking powder and salt into the whisked mixture, gently fold it into the batter until evenly blended.
9 Turn the batter into the prepared tin and level the surface. Bake for about 20 minutes until the cake is set and golden. Cool on a wire rack.
10 Reserve 8 hazelnuts; spread the rest on a baking sheet and heat in the oven for 10 minutes. Rub off the skins and either grind the nuts in an electric blender or pound to a powder with a rolling pin.
11 Reserve 8 apricot halves; lift the rest from the syrup and rub through a sieve to make a purée. Stir 2-3 tablespoons brandy into the purée. If necessary, a little sugar syrup may be added to thin the purée sufficiently to make a fairly soft sauce.
12 Whip the creams until softly thick then flavour with the icing sugar and vanilla essence.
13 Cut the cake in half horizontally through the centre. Lift the top layer on to a baking sheet and spread thinly with some cream and then sprinkle with some of the nuts. Pipe (or spoon) 8 whirls of cream, and place alternately with the reserved apricot halves round the edge of the cake.
14 Stand the bottom layer on a large flat plate and spread with the apricot purée.
15 Mix the remaining hazelnuts with the remaining cream, sweeten to taste if necessary then spread over the apricot purée.
16 Carefully slip the top layer of the gâteau from the baking sheet on to the bottom layer, and decorate each whirl of cream with one of the reserved hazelnuts.

APRICOT AND CHERRY SHORTCAKE

(Makes one 19 cm/7½in three-layer shortcake)

225 g (8oz) self-raising flour
pinch of salt
100 g (4oz) butter
finely grated rind ½ lemon
50 g (2oz) castor sugar
1 egg, beaten
2 tablespoons milk
a little egg white
25 g (1oz) flaked almonds
FILLING
2 egg yolks
50 g (2oz) castor sugar
25 g (1oz) plain flour
250 ml (½ pint) milk
¼ teaspoon almond essence
25 g (1oz) butter
350 g (12oz) ripe apricots, stoned and halved
225 g (8oz) ripe cherries, stoned

1 Preheat a moderate oven (180 deg C, 350 deg F, Gas 4), centre and above centre shelves. Grease three baking sheets.
2 Sift the flour and salt into a bowl. Rub in the butter finely.
3 Mix in the lemon rind and sugar, then the egg and milk, to make a fairly soft, but not sticky dough.
4 Divide the dough in three and roll out on a lightly floured surface to make three 19 cm (7½in) rounds. Lift carefully on to baking sheets and mark the edges with the prongs of a fork.
5 Bake two rounds for 15-20 minutes. Remove from the oven and leave to cool on the sheets.
6 Meanwhile, brush remaining round with egg white and sprinkle over flaked almonds. Bake as the other two rounds and leave to cool. (This round is for the top.)
7 **To make the filling:** Place the egg yolks and sugar in a bowl and whisk until thick and creamy. Beat in the flour and one tablespoon of the milk.
8 Put remaining milk to heat. When nearly boiling, gradually whisk it into the egg mixture. Return the mixture to the saucepan, and bring to the boil, stirring constantly. Remove from heat and beat in the essence and butter. Leave until cold, giving it an occasional stir to prevent a skin forming.
9 Spread about half the filling on one plain round.

Reserve 7 apricot halves for decoration and roughly chop remainder; spread over the filling.

10 Spread remaining filling over the other plain round. Reserve 7 cherries for decoration and chop remainder; spread over filling.

11 Place the cherry-topped round on the apricot-topped round. Cover with the almond round. Decorate with reserved apricot halves with cherries in the centre. Serve on the day it is made.

APRICOT AND ALMOND GATEAU

(Serves 6-8)
SPONGE CAKE
1 level teaspoon each of plain flour and castor
   sugar for coating tin
3 large eggs
75 g (3oz) castor sugar
75 g (3oz) plain flour
DECORATION
400 ml (¾ pint) water
75 g (3oz) castor sugar
450 g (1lb) fresh apricots
150 ml (5fl oz) double cream
2 drops almond essence
50 g (2oz) ground almonds
2 heaped tablespoons apricot jam

1 Preheat a moderate oven (180 deg C, 350 deg F, Gas 4), centre shelf. Grease an 18 cm (7in) round cake tin and add the teaspoon flour and sugar.

2 Separate the eggs and whisk the whites until very stiff.

3 Bring a pan of hot water to the boil and remove from heat. Put the yolks and sugar in a bowl over the hot water pan, whisk until thick, fluffy and much paler. Remove from heat, add the egg whites and continue whisking until thick.

4 Sift in the flour and fold it in very lightly, using a metal spoon, until it is evenly mixed. Turn into the cake tin and level the surface.

5 Bake for 25-30 minutes until brown and drawing away from the edge of the tin. Turn out carefully on to a wire rack, leave until cold.

6 To decorate: Heat the water with the sugar in a saucepan until the sugar has dissolved. Boil for 2 minutes. Lower the heat and add the apricots to the pan. Poach very gently, shaking the pan occasionally, until the fruit is just tender but not mushy, about 5-10 minutes, depending on ripeness.

7 Lift out the fruit with a draining spoon and cool. Boil the syrup for 5 minutes to reduce it.

8 Place the cream and almond essence in a small bowl and whisk until just stiff. Fold in the ground almonds.

9 Cut the cake in half horizontally and place the lower piece on a serving plate. Spread with about two-thirds of the almond cream.

10 Halve the apricots and remove the stones and any stalks. Reserving the best halves for the top of the cake, cut the rest into pieces and arrange on the cream.

11 Sandwich with the other half of the cake and spread the top with the remaining cream. Arrange the reserved apricot halves on top of the cake, and cut side down.

12 Place the apricot jam in a saucepan and add a tablespoon of the apricot syrup. Simmer for one minute, cool slightly and spoon over the fruit to glaze. Keep cool until ready to serve.

HONEY SPONGE WITH BRANDY CONES

(Cuts into 8 slices)
SPONGE CAKE
175 g (6oz) butter or margarine
75 g (3oz) castor sugar
75 g (3oz) thick honey
3 eggs, separated
175 g (6oz) self-raising flour
¾ level teaspoon ground cinnamon
1-2 tablespoons milk or brandy

BRANDY CONES
50 g (2oz) butter or margarine
25 g (1oz) soft brown or demerara sugar
75 g (3oz) golden syrup
50 g (2oz) plain flour
1 level teaspoon ground ginger

FILLING
125 g (4oz) orange marmalade
150 ml (5fl oz) double cream

1 Preheat a moderately hot oven (190 deg C, 375 deg F, Gas 5), centre shelf. Grease two 19 cm (7½in) sandwich tins and line the bases with greased greaseproof paper.

2 Place the butter, sugar and honey in a mixing bowl and beat well together until creamy. Beat in the egg yolks.

3 Sift in the flour with the cinnamon and fold in with the milk or brandy to make a smooth mixture.

4 Whisk the egg whites until stiff. Lightly stir in a tablespoon and then fold in the rest until evenly mixed. Divide the mixture evenly between the tins and level the surface.

5 Bake for about 25 minutes until just firm to the touch in the centre.

6 Loosen the edges with a knife and turn out carefully on to a wire rack to cool.

7 To make the brandy cones: Preheat a warm oven (170 deg C, 325 deg F, Gas 3), centre shelf. Grease two baking sheets.

8 Place the butter in a small saucepan and add the sugar and syrup. Heat gently until the sugar has dissolved.

9 Remove from the heat and sift in the flour and ginger. Stir well to mix.

10 Place small teaspoonsful of the mixture on one baking sheet, well apart to allow for spreading. Do not cook more than 6 on one sheet.

11 Place in the oven for 8-10 minutes until the biscuits are a rich dark golden brown. If they are undercooked they will be chewy, not crunchy.

12 Remove from the oven and put in the second sheet of biscuits.

13 Carefully ease the biscuits off the baking sheet with a palette knife, and make into cone shapes. If they become

Honey sponge with brandy cones, *see opposite*

35

too firm on the baking sheet return to the oven to warm for a minute. (Any broken or uneven ones may be used for crushing later.)

14 To decorate: Cut each cake across horizontally into two equal layers and sandwich together with marmalade.

15 Whip the cream until thick. Spread half round the sides of the cake.

16 Reserving 8 of the best brandy cones, lightly crush enough to go round the side of the cake. Gently roll the cake in the crushed biscuit. (Keep any remaining cones in an airtight container to fill with cream or to serve with ice-cream.)

17 Spread remainder of the cream on top of the cake. Place the 8 cones on top radiating from the centre.

Note: *The cake and cones could be made the day before they are wanted, but do keep the cones in an airtight container otherwise they will go tacky. The cake should all be eaten at one serving — if not, remove the cones.*

See picture on page 35

PINEAPPLE AND CREAM GATEAU

(Serves 8)

225 g (8oz) soft margarine
225 g (8oz) castor sugar
4 eggs
225 g (8oz) self-raising flour
341 g (12oz) can pineapple rings
1 level tablespoon custard powder
150 ml (5fl oz) single cream
150 ml (5fl oz) double cream
2 large bars chocolate flake
6 Maraschino or glacé cherries

1 Preheat a moderate oven (180 deg C, 350 deg F, Gas 4), centre shelf. Brush two 20 cm (8in) sandwich tins with oil or melted fat. Line the bases with rounds of greased greaseproof paper.

2 Mix the margarine, sugar, eggs and flour in a bowl until well blended.

3 Divide the mixture between the tins and spread evenly with the back of a spoon.

4 Bake for ½ hour until golden brown and firm to the touch. Leave to cool in the tins for 5 minutes. Loosen the edges with a round bladed knife, turn out, remove paper and leave on a wire rack until cold.

5 Drain the pineapple rings, reserving the syrup in a measuring jug (make up to 150 ml/5fl oz with water if necessary).

6 Blend the custard powder with a little of the syrup in a saucepan. Stir in the remaining syrup. Bring to the boil, stirring, remove from heat and leave until cold. Chop 2 pineapple rings and add to the mixture. Sandwich the sponges together with the pineapple filling.

7 Place the single and double creams in a basin. Whisk until the cream just holds its shape. Place 3 rounded tablespoons cream in a piping bag fitted with a large star vegetable pipe, whisk the remaining cream until stiff. Spread some cream around the side of the cake.

8 Lightly crush the chocolate flake reserving a few pieces for decoration. Hold the top and bottom of the cake between the hands and press the side on to the crushed chocolate flake to coat.

9 Place the cake on a flat serving dish and spread the top with the remaining cream. Arrange the remaining 6 pineapple rings on top of the cake. Pipe whirls of cream in the centres and round the outsides of the pineapple rings.

10 Decorate the centre whirls with cherries and the outer whirls with the remaining chocolate pieces. Keep cool until ready to serve.

ORANGE MERINGUE CAKE

(Cuts into 6-8 slices)

125 g (4oz) butter or margarine
125 g (4oz) castor sugar
3 egg yolks
grated rind ½ orange
125 g (4oz) self-raising flour
3-4 tablespoons orange juice
TOPPING
3 egg whites
pinch of salt
175 g (6oz) castor sugar
grated rind 1½ oranges
2 tablespoons lemon or orange curd
312 g (11oz) can mandarin segments

1 Preheat a moderately hot oven (190 deg C, 375 deg F, Gas 5), shelf above centre. Grease a 20 cm (8in) round cake tin on the base only.

2 Cream the butter and sugar in a medium-sized bowl until light and fluffy. Beat in the egg yolks one at a time, and the orange rind.

3 Sift the flour, fold into the creamed mixture, using a metal spoon. Add the orange juice carefully, a tablespoon at a time to make a soft dropping consistency.

4 Turn the mixture into the prepared tin and smooth over the top.

5 Bake for about ½ hour or until the cake springs back when lightly pressed with the fingertip. Remove from the oven, turn out of the tin and cool slightly on a wire rack while making the topping.

6 Reduce oven temperature to cool (150 deg C, 300 deg F, Gas 2), centre shelf.

7 To make the topping: Whisk the egg whites with the salt until stiff and standing in peaks. Gradually add the sugar, whisking well after each addition. Fold in the orange rind.

8 Spread the lemon or orange curd over the cake and top with a few drained mandarin segments. Cover with the prepared meringue in an even layer.

9 Transfer the cake to a baking sheet and bake for a further ½ hour until the meringue is set and lightly brown.

10 Cool on a wire rack and decorate with the remaining drained mandarin segments.

Note: *This cake is best eaten the day it is made.*

ORANGE JEWEL CAKE

(Makes one 25 cm/10in round cake)
350 g (12oz) margarine
350 g (12oz) castor sugar
6 eggs
350 g (12oz) self-raising flour
grated rind 1 orange
grated rind 1 lemon
FILLING AND TOPPING
25 g (1oz) flaked almonds
2 oranges
100 g (4oz) granulated sugar
4 tablespoons water
275 g (10oz) butter or margarine
725 g (1lb 10oz) icing sugar
orange food colouring

1 Preheat a moderately hot oven (190 deg C, 375 deg F, Gas 5), centre shelf. Grease a 25 cm (10in) round cake tin and line with greased greaseproof paper.

2 Cream the margarine and castor sugar until light and fluffy. Gradually beat in the eggs one at a time, adding a tablespoon of flour with the last egg.

3 Sift remaining flour and fold into the creamed mixture with the orange and lemon rinds.

4 Turn the mixture into the tin and level the surface. Bake for about 1 hour 15 minutes until golden and springy to the touch.

5 Leave to cool in the tin about 10 minutes before turning out on to a wire rack. When cold, store in an airtight container until required.

6 **To make the filling and topping:** While the cake is baking, the flaked almonds may be browned in the lower part of the oven for about 5 minutes. Alternatively, they may be browned under a medium grill. Allow to cool.

7 Using a potato peeler, peel the rind from the oranges, then snip it into very small pieces with scissors. Place a piece of greaseproof paper on a baking sheet and brush with a little oil.

8 Place the granulated sugar and water in a small saucepan. Heat slowly, stirring, until sugar is dissolved. Bring to the boil and boil until it turns a light golden colour. Immediately add the orange rind, give a quick stir and pour on to the oiled paper. Leave until set, then break into small pieces.

9 Cream the butter until soft, then beat in 550 g (1lb 4oz) of the icing sugar and the juice of one orange. Beat until

soft and fluffy. Divide in half. Beat half the sugared orange rind into one half.

10 Cut the cake into three layers horizontally and sandwich together with the orange rind butter icing.

11 Spread about half the remaining butter icing round the side of the cake and press the toasted almonds on to this. Place on a cake board or large plate.

12 Place remaining butter icing in teaspoonsful around the top edge of the cake and join together to form a circle. Using a fork, make a rough pattern on this.

13 Sift the remaining icing sugar into a bowl and beat in about 1½-2 tablespoons orange juice with a few drops of colouring, until it thickly coats the back of a spoon.

14 Pour on top of the cake and spread to butter icing circle. Sprinkle remaining sugared orange rind on to butter icing circle. Leave to set.

ORANGE CAKE WITH CHOCOLATE FUDGE TOPPING

(Makes a deep 20 cm/8in cake)
200 g (8oz) soft margarine
200 g (8oz) castor sugar
4 eggs
200 g (8oz) self-raising flour
½ level teaspoon mixed spice
pinch of salt
grated rind 1 orange
1-2 tablespoons orange juice
FILLING
312 g (11oz) can mandarins
150 ml (5fl oz) double cream
ICING
200 g (7oz) granulated sugar
125 ml (4fl oz) milk
25 g (1oz) butter
25 g (1oz) plain chocolate
1 tablespoon single cream or milk

1 Preheat a moderate oven (180 deg C, 350 deg F, Gas 4), centre shelf. Grease two 20 cm (8in) sandwich tins and line the bases with greased greaseproof paper.

2 Cream the margarine and castor sugar until light and fluffy. Gradually beat in the eggs one at a time, adding a tablespoon of flour with the last egg.

3 Sift remaining flour, mixed spice and salt and stir into the creamed mixture with the orange rind and juice.

4 Divide the mixture between the tins and level the surfaces. Bake for about 45 minutes until golden and springy to the touch.

5 Turn out on to a wire rack, remove the paper and allow to cool. When cold, store in an airtight container until required.

6 **To make the filling:** Drain the mandarins really well (juice can be used in a jelly). Whisk the cream until thick then fold in the mandarins. Sandwich the cakes together with the cream and mandarin mixture.

7 **To make the icing:** Put the sugar, milk, butter and chocolate in a small strong pan. Stir over very gentle heat until the ingredients have melted. Cover with a lid, bring

to the boil and continue to boil gently for 2 minutes.

8 Remove lid from pan and continue boiling until 115 deg C (235-8 deg F) is reached (soft ball stage – a drop of mixture will form a pliable ball in cold water), this takes about 7 minutes.

9 Remove the pan from the heat at once. When the bubbles die down, add the cream or milk. Allow the mixture to cool for a few more minutes then beat with a wooden spoon until it begins to lose its sheen and thicken. When thick, pour at once over the top of the cake, swirl icing into a pattern with a spoon. Leave to set.

Note: For a smaller cake make up half cake mixture and bake in 15-18 cm (6-7in) sandwich tins for about ½ hour.

HER MAJESTY'S GATEAU

(Serves 10)

4 lemons
200 g (7oz) granulated sugar
250 ml (½ pint) water
two 25 cm (10in) sponge flan cases
40 g (1½oz) cornflour
400 ml (¾ pint) milk
50 g (2oz) butter
4 large eggs
225 g (8oz) castor sugar

1 Squeeze the juice from one of the lemons.

2 Slowly heat 75 g (3oz) of the granulated sugar in the water, stirring from time to time until dissolved, then remove pan from heat and add the lemon juice.

3 Place one of the flan cases on a large ovenproof serving dish (or a baking sheet covered in kitchen foil) and sprinkle it all over with half the lemon syrup.

4 Finely grate the rind and squeeze the juice from the remaining 3 lemons.

5 Blend the cornflour with the milk in a saucepan, then stir over a medium heat until the sauce comes to the boil and thickens. Add the remaining granulated sugar, butter, lemon rind and juice.

7 Return the pan to a medium heat and stir briskly for a few minutes until the sauce is evenly blended, then remove from heat and cool slightly.

8 Separate the egg whites from the yolks, stir the yolks into the lemon sauce and pour into the moistened flan case. Turn the other flan case upside down on to the lemon filling and sprinkle it evenly with the remaining lemon syrup. Cover with foil and leave aside overnight.

9 Preheat a moderate oven (180 deg C, 350 deg F, Gas 4), centre shelf.

10 Whisk the egg whites until stiff and standing in peaks, then add the castor sugar, a level tablespoon at a time, whisking well after each addition to make a really thick meringue.

11 Using as little of the meringue mixture as possible, completely cover the moist flan cake so that none of the sponge shows through. Smooth the meringue over the cake, then use the remaining meringue to surround the edges and decorate the top of the cake by lifting it into peaks with a knife. Alternatively you can, if you like, pipe

the meringue into a decorative pattern.

12 Bake the gâteau for 30-40 minutes until the meringue is crisp and just turning golden brown. Allow to cool. Serve with cream. It is best served on the day it is made.

SICILIAN LAYER CAKE

(Cuts into 10-12 slices)

3 large eggs
125 g (4½oz) castor sugar
125 g (4½oz) self-raising flour, sifted
FILLING
225 g (8oz) full fat soft cream cheese
50 g (2oz) icing sugar, sifted
100 g (4oz) mixed peel
50 g (2oz) chocolate drops for cooking
2 tablespoons Cointreau or other orange liqueur
TOPPING
225 g (8oz) full fat soft cream cheese
50 g (2oz) icing sugar, sifted
40 g (1½oz) chocolate drops for cooking
1 glacé cherry
angelica

1 Preheat a moderate oven (180 deg C, 350 deg F, Gas 4), centre shelf. Lightly oil a 2-litre (3½-pint) loaf tin.

2 Place the eggs in a bowl with the castor sugar and place bowl over a pan of boiling water, whisk until really thick and the whisk leaves a trail in the mixture. Remove bowl from the heat and continue whisking until the mixture has cooled.

3 Gradually fold in the sifted flour with a metal spoon, pour into the prepared loaf tin.

4 Cook for 35-40 minutes until light pressure with the fingertips leaves no mark.

5 Turn out on to a wire rack and leave until cool.

6 To make the filling: Beat the cream cheese with the icing sugar until smooth, stir in the mixed peel and the chocolate drops.

7 Cut cooled cake into three equal layers lengthwise and sprinkle each sponge with a little Cointreau.

8 Place the bottom sponge on a serving dish or board, spread with half the filling, top with the centre sponge. Spread over remainder of filling, cover with remaining sponge. Press cake gently.

9 To make the topping: Blend the cream cheese and icing sugar together and spread evenly over the top and sides of the cake.

10 Melt chocolate drops in a small bowl placed over a pan of hot water, then trickle the chocolate over the top of the cake.

11 Cut the glacé cherry into quarters and arrange over the cake, with angelica cut into diamond shapes and placed as leaves on each side of the cherry quarters.

12 Chill before serving. Serve cut in thin slices.

See picture opposite

Sicilian Layer Cake, *see opposite*

NUSSKUCHEN

(Serves 8)

150 g (5oz) hazelnuts
50 g (2oz) fresh white breadcrumbs
5 eggs
150 g (5oz) castor sugar
a few drops vanilla essence
2 heaped tablespoons apricot jam
DECORATION
175 g (6oz) icing sugar
2 rounded teaspoons instant coffee powder
a little very hot water
25 g (1oz) hazelnuts

1 Preheat a moderately hot oven (190 deg C, 375 deg F, Gas 5), centre shelf. Grease an 18 cm (7in) round cake tin and lightly coat with flour, shaking out any excess.
2 Place the hazelnuts under a moderate grill until the skins are flaking off and then rub them off between the palms of the hands.
3 Grind the nuts until fine and place in a bowl with the breadcrumbs.
4 Separate the egg yolks from the whites, placing them in different bowls.
5 Add the sugar and vanilla essence to the yolks and cream with a wooden spoon until the mixture is thick and pale.
6 Whisk the egg whites until stiff and standing in peaks, then fold into the creamed mixture with the nuts and crumbs, using a large metal spoon.
7 When evenly folded through, turn into the cake tin and level the surface with a palette knife.
8 Cook for about 35 minutes until risen and lightly browned. Remove from the oven and leave to cool in the tin for a few minutes, then turn the cake out on to a wire rack to finish cooling. Cut in half horizontally.
9 Spread the lower half of the cake with apricot jam and sandwich the cake together. Place on a wire rack for icing.
10 Sift the icing sugar into a bowl. Place the coffee in a cup and blend with one tablespoon very hot water. Stir into the icing sugar with a very little extra water to give a smooth thick icing.
11 Spread over the top and sides of the cake to coat it evenly. Arrange the remaining hazelnuts (unskinned) round the edge to decorate and leave to set.
12 Lift the cake on to a serving place when icing is set.

MAGDA TORTE

(Serves 8-10)

2 level teaspoons instant coffee powder
1 teaspoon boiling water
50 g (2oz) plain chocolate
3 eggs
100 g (4oz) soft margarine
75 g (3oz) self-raising flour
100 g (4oz) castor sugar
25 g (1oz) ground almonds

FILLING
75 g (3oz) icing sugar
25 g (1oz) cocoa
75 g (3oz) butter or margarine
2 tablespoons brandy
150 ml (5fl oz) strong black coffee

DECORATION
150 ml (5fl oz) double cream
1 egg white
25 g (1oz) icing sugar
chocolate coffee beans

1 Preheat a moderately hot oven (190 deg C, 375 deg F, Gas 5), centre shelf. Grease a fairly deep 20 cm (8in) sandwich tin and line with greased greaseproof paper, or grease a 1¼-litre (2-pint) metal ring mould.
2 Dissolve the instant coffee powder in the water. Break the chocolate into a small bowl and stand it over a pan of boiling water to melt.
3 Separate one of the eggs and whisk the white stiffly. Place the soft margarine, flour, castor sugar and 2 remaining eggs in a bowl and beat together for 2 minutes then fold in the ground almonds with the stiffly-beaten egg white.
4 Divide the mixture in half. Fold the dissolved coffee into one half and the melted chocolate into the other, then place spoonfuls of the different mixtures alternately in the prepared tin.
5 Cook the cake for 35-40 minutes until well risen and firm to touch. Cool slightly in the tin, then turn out on to a wire rack. When cold, cut into 3 layers.
6 **To make the filling:** Sift the icing sugar with the cocoa into a bowl, and cream them with the butter until soft and smooth, then beat in the egg yolk left over from the cake.
7 Mix the brandy with the coffee.
8 Wash the tin the cake was cooked in and line with cling film (or foil). Place the first layers of the case in the tin and moisten it with a third of the coffee-brandy mixture.
9 Spread half the chocolate butter icing over the moistened cake then top with next layer of cake, moisten this with another third of the coffee, spread with a final layer of filling, place last layer of cake on top and moisten with the remaining coffee.
10 Cover the top of the cake with a piece of foil or film and leave it overnight in a cold place.
11 **To decorate:** Turn the cake out on to a serving plate Whip the double cream until it is thick, whisk the egg white until stiff and fold it into the cream with the icing sugar. Use about half the cream to cover the cake and the

remainder to pipe whirls on top. Decorate each with a chocolate coffee bean.

TIPSY PUFF RING

(Serves 4)
65 g (2½oz) plain flour
pinch of salt
50 g (2oz) butter or margarine
150 ml (5fl oz) water
2 eggs
FILLING
2 egg yolks
50 g (2oz) castor sugar
25 g (1oz) plain flour
150 ml (5fl oz) milk
25 g (1oz) butter
1 tablespoon rum
1 egg white
icing sugar

1 Preheat a moderately hot oven (200 deg C, 400 deg F, Gas 6), centre shelf. Grease a baking sheet and mark a 20 cm (8in) circle.
2 Sift the flour and salt on to a plate.
3 Place the fat and water in a pan. Heat gently until the fat melts then bring to the boil. Remove from heat and quickly add the flour and salt all at once. Beat until smooth and cool slightly.
4 Lightly whisk the eggs and very gradually beat into the paste, beating well after each addition to form a shiny, smooth mixture.
5 Place in a forcing bag (without a tube) and pipe a 20 cm (8in) ring on the baking sheet. Alternatively, place the mixture in small teaspoonsful on a marked circle on the baking sheet, then smooth them together with a knife to form a ring.
6 Bake for ½ hour, then reduce oven heat to moderate (180 deg C, 350 deg F, Gas 4). Remove from oven and cut a few slits on the inner edge of the ring. Return to the oven for a further 10 minutes. Then cool on a wire rack.
7 To make the filling: Place the egg yolks and one tablespoon of the measured sugar in a basin and beat until thick, creamy and pale. Beat in the flour and one tablespoon of the measured milk. Bring remaining milk to boil, then slowly add to the egg mixture, beating well. Return to the saucepan and bring to the boil, stirring continuously, simmer for one minute. Remove from heat and beat in the butter and rum. Cover and leave until quite cold.
8 Whisk the egg white until stiff, then whisk in one more tablespoon from the measured sugar. Fold in remaining sugar. Whisk sauce, then carefully fold in the whisked egg white and sugar.
9 Split the ring and spoon in filling. Sandwich together, dredge with icing sugar and serve on the same day.

ADVOCAAT DESSERT CAKE

(Cuts into about 8-10 portions)
175 g (6oz) plain flour
1 level teaspoon baking powder
175 g (6oz) butter, slightly softened
175 g (6oz) castor sugar
4 eggs, separated
225 ml (8fl oz) Advocaat
SAUCE
150 ml (5fl oz) double cream
3 tablespoons Advocaat

1 Preheat a moderate oven (180 deg C, 350 deg F, Gas 4), centre shelf. Brush base and sides of a 20 cm (8in) spring form pan or loose-based cake tin with a little melted butter, then dust the tin lightly with a little flour.
2 Sift together the flour and baking powder twice into a bowl. In a separate bowl, cream the butter and sugar until they become quite light and fluffy.
3 Beat in the egg yolks, followed by two-thirds of the Advocaat with one tablespoon of the flour.
4 Whisk the egg whites to a firm but not over-stiff snow. Using a spatula, gently fold into the creamed mixture alternately with the rest of the Advocaat and flour.
5 When smooth and evenly combined, transfer the mixture to the prepared tin and bake for one hour.
6 Cool 5 minutes then unclip the sides of pan or carefully ease out of tin. Cut the dessert cake into wedges and serve warm with the cream sauce, made by beating the double cream until softly stiff then folding in the Advocaat.

Note: *This is a very rich, moist cake.*

See picture on page 70

41

chapter 5
Small Cakes and Buns

**The little cakes to make in batches of a dozen or more.
There are buns and rock cakes to make for family teas;
iced specials for party days**

DATE SQUARES

(Makes 9 squares)
125 g (4oz) dates
75 ml (3fl oz) boiling water
½ teaspoon lemon juice
50 g (2oz) butter or margarine
50 g (2oz) castor sugar
75 g (3oz) self-raising flour
pinch of salt
1 tablespoon water
¼ level teaspoon bicarbonate of soda
125 g (4oz) rolled oats

1 Preheat a moderate oven (180 deg C, 350 deg F, Gas 4), centre shelf. Lightly grease an 18 cm (7in) square sandwich tin.
2 Stone the dates if necessary.
3 Put the boiling water, dates and lemon juice together in a saucepan, and cook gently until soft and mashed, for about 10 minutes.
4 Meanwhile, cream together the butter and sugar. Stir in the flour and salt.
5 Mix together the water and bicarbonate of soda and stir into the mixture. Add the oats and mix well.
6 Divide the mixture into two parts. Put one part into the prepared tin and press down evenly. Spread with the cooked dates.
7 Distribute the remaining mixture evenly over the top, in small lumps.
8 Bake for 45 minutes, until lightly golden. Cool slightly, cut into 9 squares, and leave in the tin to finish cooling.
See picture opposite, top right

BRAN MUFFINS

(Makes 10-12)
125 g (4oz) self-raising flour
½ level teaspoon salt
50 g (2oz) soft brown sugar
50 g (2oz) bran
1 level teaspoon bicarbonate of soda
175 ml (6fl oz) milk
25 g (1oz) cooking oil
25 g (1oz) golden syrup
1 large egg, beaten

1 Preheat a moderately hot oven (200 deg C, 400 deg F, Gas 6), shelf above centre. Grease 10-12 deep bun tins.
2 Sift the flour and salt into a medium-sized bowl. Mix in the sugar and bran.
3 Dissolve the bicarbonate of soda in milk, add the oil, golden syrup and beaten egg.
4 Make a well in the centre of the dry ingredients, pour in the liquid and stir quickly with a wooden spoon until just mixed, to make a soft dropping consistency.
5 Fill the bun tins two-thirds full.
6 Bake 15-20 minutes until brown and firm to the touch.
7 Remove the muffins and leave on a wire rack until they are just warm. Serve with butter and honey.
See picture opposite, top left

*It is important to follow **either** the metric **or** the imperial weights and measures in any one recipe*

Top: **Bran Muffins** *(left), see opposite;* **Date Squares** *(right), see opposite; Above:* **Saffron Rock Buns,** *page 44*

SAFFRON ROCK BUNS

(Makes 12)

1 small packet saffron strands
50 ml (2fl oz) boiling water
1 egg, beaten
225 g (8oz) self-raising flour
pinch of salt
25 g (1oz) lard or cooking fat
50 g (2oz) butter or margarine
75 g (3oz) granulated sugar
75 g (3oz) sultanas
25 g (1oz) chopped mixed peel

1 Put the saffron in a measuring jug and pour on the boiling water. Soak for at least 2 hours or overnight.
2 Preheat a moderately hot oven (190 deg C, 375 deg F, Gas 5), shelf above centre. Grease a baking sheet.
3 Drain the saffron into the beaten egg.
4 Sift the flour and salt into a bowl. Cut in the fats and rub in until the mixture resembles fine breadcrumbs.
5 Stir in the sugar, sultanas and peel and mix to a stiff mixture with the saffron egg mixture.
6 Divide the mixture into 12 rough heaps on the baking sheet. Bake for about 20 minutes until firm to touch and golden brown. Cool on a wire rack.
See picture on page 43, below

MARBLED CUP CAKES

(Makes 12)

50 g (2oz) butter or margarine
125 g (4oz) castor sugar
2 large eggs, beaten
125 g (4oz) self-raising flour, sifted
2 tablespoons milk
50 g (2oz) cooking chocolate
ICING
50 g (2oz) cooking chocolate
100 g (4oz) icing sugar
1 tablespoon warm water
extra chocolate for grating

1 Preheat a moderately hot oven (190 deg C, 375 deg F, Gas 5), shelf above centre. Place 12 paper cake cases in hollows of tartlet tins.
2 Cream the butter and sugar until light and fluffy. Gradually beat in the eggs, beating well after each addition.
3 Fold in half the flour with a metal spoon, then the milk and then the remaining flour.
4 Break the chocolate into pieces and place in a small bowl set over a pan of hot water. Leave until melted.
5 Divide the cake mixture in two and place one half in a separate bowl. Stir the melted chocolate into one half.
6 Place spoonfuls of each mixture into the prepared paper cases, fill about two-thirds full. Swirl mixtures together slightly to obtain a marbled effect.

7 Bake for 15-20 minutes, or until firm when pressed lightly with the fingertips. Cool on a wire rack.
8 To make the icing: Melt the chocolate over hot water. Sift the icing sugar into a small bowl and mix with the warm water. Stir in the melted chocolate.
9 When cool, spread the icing on the tops of the cakes and sprinkle grated chocolate over to decorate.

SPICED CUP CAKES

(Makes 14)

75 g (3oz) butter or margarine
75 g (3oz) castor sugar
1 egg, beaten
125 g (4oz) self-raising flour
½ level teaspoon ground cinnamon
¼ level teaspoon ground black pepper
¼ level teaspoon ground cloves
¼ teaspoon vanilla essence
2-3 tablespoons milk or water
ICING
150 g (5oz) icing sugar
¼-½ level teaspoon ground cinnamon
about 2 tablespoons hot water

1 Preheat a moderately hot oven (190 deg C, 375 deg F, Gas 5), shelf above centre. Place 14 paper cake cases on a baking sheet.
2 Cream butter and sugar until light and fluffy, gradually beat in the egg, beating well after each addition.
3 Sift in the flour, cinnamon, black pepper and cloves, add the vanilla essence, mix well, and add enough milk or water to make a soft dropping consistency.
4 Divide mixture between the cake cases. Bake 15-20 minutes until firm to the touch. Cool on a wire rack.
5 To make the icing: Sift the icing sugar and cinnamon into a bowl. Mix to a thick coating consistency with the hot water.
6 Spread the icing over the cup cakes and leave to set.

HAZELNUT CHERRY CUP CAKES

(Makes 24)

125 g (4oz) butter or margarine
125 g (4oz) castor sugar
2 eggs, beaten
50 g (2oz) chopped roasted hazelnuts
150 g (5oz) self-raising flour
149 g (5¼oz) jar Maraschino-flavoured cocktail cherries, drained and liquid reserved
1 tablespoon milk
ICING
350 g (12oz) icing sugar, sifted
reserved cherry liquid
pink food colouring

1 Preheat a moderately hot oven (190 deg C, 375 deg F, Gas 5), towards top and centre shelves. Place 24 paper cake cases in hollows of tartlet tins.

2 Cream the butter and sugar until soft and pale. Gradually beat in the eggs, stir in the hazelnuts. Fold in the flour with 2 tablespoons liquor from the cherry jar and the milk, until evenly mixed.

3 Place teaspoonsful of the mixture in paper cases dividing the mixture as evenly as possible. Bake for 15-20 minutes until lightly brown and just firm to touch. Lift on to a wire rack to cool.

4 To make the icing: Add sufficient cherry liquid to the icing sugar to make a smooth thick paste. Add a few drops of pink colouring. Spread on the cakes. Dry 24 cherries, place one on each cake.

ELFIN CAKES

(Makes 12)

75 g (3oz) butter or margarine
75 g (3oz) castor sugar
2 eggs
75 g (3oz) self-raising flour, sifted
25 g (1oz) ground rice
50 g (2oz) chopped mixed peel
ICING
75 g (3oz) icing sugar, sifted
1 tablespoon water
3 glacé cherries, quartered

1 Preheat a moderate oven (180 deg C, 350 deg F, Gas 4), centre shelf. Lightly grease 12 tartlet tins or place 12 paper cake cases on a baking sheet.

2 Cream the butter and sugar, until light and fluffy.

3 Separate the yolks from the whites of the eggs, and beat the yolks into the creamed mixture.

4 Fold in the flour and add the ground rice. Stir in the chopped peel.

5 Whisk the egg whites until stiff, and fold into the mixture.

6 Spoon into the prepared tins or paper cases, bake for 15-20 minutes, until risen and lightly coloured.

7 Turn out to cool on a wire rack, or allow to cool in the paper cake cases.

8 To make the icing: Mix the icing sugar with the water to a fairly stiff consistency. Spread over the tops of the cakes and decorate each one with a quarter cherry.

CHOCORANGE BUNS

(Makes 16-18)

125 g (4oz) soft margarine
125 g (4oz) castor sugar
2 eggs
125 g (4oz) self-raising flour
1 level teaspoon baking powder
finely grated rind 1 orange
50 g (2oz) chocolate drops for cooking
ICING
125 g (4oz) icing sugar
juice 1 orange
orange food colouring (optional)
25 g (1oz) chocolate drops for cooking

1 Preheat a moderately hot oven (190 deg C, 375 deg F, Gas 5), shelf above centre. Arrange 16-18 paper cake cases on a baking sheet.

2 Place the margarine, sugar and eggs in a mixing bowl and sift the flour and baking powder in together. Add the orange rind.

3 Beat well until soft and creamy, about 2-3 minutes. Fold in the chocolate drops until evenly mixed.

4 Using a teaspoon, half fill the paper cases with the mixture. Bake for 15-20 minutes until just firm to the touch. Lift on to a wire rack to cool before making the orange icing.

5 To make the icing: Sift the icing sugar into a small bowl and add just enough orange juice to make a smooth icing. If liked, add a drop of orange colouring.

6 Spread the orange icing over the tops of the buns to cover. Decorate with a few chocolate drops. Or stand the chocolate drops in a cup over hot water until melted, then place a little chocolate on top of each bun and, using the tip of a knife, make a rough star shape.

MOCHA CAKES

(Makes 12)

175 g (6oz) butter or margarine
125 g (4oz) castor sugar
150 g (5oz) plain flour
50 g (2oz) cornflour
25 g (1oz) cocoa
¼ teaspoon vanilla essence
ICING
25 g (1oz) butter or margarine
50 g (2oz) icing sugar
1 level teaspoon instant coffee
chocolate drops or a little grated chocolate for decoration

1 Place 12 paper cake cases on a baking sheet.

2 Beat the butter and sugar until creamy.

3 Add the flour and sift in the cornflour and cocoa together. Add the vanilla essence and mix well.

4 Place the mixture in a large piping bag, fitted with a large star tube. Pipe around the edge of the paper cases, leaving holes in the centres. Chill the cakes for 15 minutes.

5 Meanwhile, preheat a warm oven (170 deg C, 325 deg F, Gas 3), centre shelf.

6 Bake the cakes for 30-35 minutes. Cool on a wire rack.

7 To make the icing: Place the butter in a small bowl and sift in the icing sugar. Dissolve the coffee in about $\frac{1}{2}$ teaspoon of hot water. Pour into the butter and sugar. Mix, and then beat the icing very well until smooth.

8 Pipe into the cake centres and decorate with chocolate drops or sprinkle with grated chocolate.

LEMON AND ALMOND MAIDS

(Makes 12 little cakes)
212 g (7½oz) packet frozen shortcrust pastry, thawed
FILLING
50 g (2oz) butter or margarine
50 g (2oz) castor sugar
1 large egg
50 g (2oz) ground almonds
drop of almond essence
1 slightly rounded tablespoon self-raising flour
grated rind ½ lemon
1 teaspoon lemon juice
ICING
150 g (5oz) icing sugar
drop of yellow food colouring
lemon juice

1 Preheat a moderately hot oven (190 deg C, 375 deg F, Gas 5), centre shelf.

2 Roll out the pastry on a lightly floured surface and, using a fluted cutter, cut out rounds to line a 12-hole tartlet tin. Re-roll trimmings to give the correct number of rounds.

3 Cream the butter and sugar until soft. Beat the egg in with the ground almonds.

4 Stir in the almond essence, flour, lemon rind and juice.

5 Divide this mixture evenly between the pastry cases, and bake for 20-25 minutes until the sponge is golden and the pastry cooked.

6 Carefully lift out of the tin and cool on a wire rack.

7 To make the icing: Sift 125 g (4oz) icing sugar into a bowl and mix with just enough cold water to make a thick icing.

8 Spread over the cakes to coat, allow to set, leaving any extra icing in the bowl.

9 Add the remaining 25 g (1oz) of icing sugar to the bowl and mix with yellow colouring and enough lemon juice to make a thick icing.

10 Fill a small piping bag and, using a fine writing tube, pipe a lattice of yellow icing over the top of each cake.

11 Leave to set before serving

See picture opposite

Top: **Lemon and Almond Maids,** *see opposite. Above:* **Devonshire-Style Strawberry Puffs,** *see page 48*

DEVONSHIRE-STYLE STRAWBERRY PUFFS

(Makes 18)
65 g (2½oz) plain flour
pinch of salt
50 g (2oz) butter or margarine
150 ml (5fl oz) water
2 eggs
FILLING
225 g (8oz) strawberries, hulled
150 ml (5fl oz) clotted cream
1 level tablespoon castor sugar
a little icing sugar

1 Preheat a moderately hot oven (200 deg C, 400 deg F, Gas 6), shelves above and below centre. Grease two baking sheets.
2 Sift the flour and salt.
3 Place the fat in a pan with the water. Heat gently until the fat melts, then bring to the boil. Remove from heat, and immediately add all the flour. Beat until smooth. Cool for 5 minutes.
4 Lightly whisk the eggs and very gradually beat into the paste, beating well after each addition to make a shiny, smooth mixture.
5 Place the mixture in 18 large teaspoonsful on baking sheets and shape into rounds.
6 Bake for 20-25 minutes. Remove from the oven and cut a slit in the side of each to allow steam to escape. Return to oven for a further 5 minutes to dry out. Allow to cool on a wire rack.
7 Mash half the strawberries in a basin with a fork. Add cream and sugar and beat with fork until thick.
8 Cut remaining strawberries in small pieces and fold into the cream mixture. Spoon the mixture into the puffs.
9 Dredge with icing sugar and serve on same day.

See picture on page 47

ORANGE CARAWAY BUNS

(Makes 12)
150 g (5oz) self-raising flour
75 g (3oz) butter or margarine
50 g (2oz) soft brown sugar
finely grated rind 1 orange
1-1½ level teaspoons caraway seeds
a little freshly grated nutmeg
1 large egg, well beaten
1 tablespoon milk
ICING
125 g (4oz) icing sugar, sifted
4 teaspoons orange juice

1 Preheat a moderate oven (180 deg C, 350 deg F, Gas 4), centre shelf. Place 12 paper cake cases in tartlet tin hollows.
2 Rub butter into flour until mixture is in fine crumbs.

3 Add the sugar, orange rind, caraway seeds, nutmeg to taste, egg and milk. Mix well to give a fairly soft mixture, divide between the paper cases.
4 Cook for 15 minutes until the buns are just firm to the touch. Then remove from the oven and allow to cool on a wire rack.
5 **To make the icing:** Mix the icing sugar with the orange juice to make a thick icing. Place teaspoonsful on the buns, allowing it to spread.

See picture on page 15

CHOCOLATE COCONUT BUNS

(Makes 12)
50 g (2oz) soft margarine
50 g (2oz) castor sugar
1 large egg
40 g (1½oz) self-raising flour
1 level tablespoon cocoa
25 g (1oz) desiccated coconut
1 tablespoon milk
jam and extra desiccated coconut

1 Preheat a moderately hot oven (200 deg C, 400 deg F, Gas 6), shelf above centre. Place 12 paper cake cases in tartlet tin hollows.
2 Cream the margarine and sugar until light and fluffy. Beat in the egg, then fold in the sifted flour, cocoa and the coconut with the milk.
3 Divide between the cases. Bake for 15 minutes until springy to the touch. Cool on a wire rack.
4 **To decorate:** Spread a little jam over the cakes and sprinkle with coconut.

CHERRY AND ALMOND STRUDEL

(Cuts into 8-12 slices)
STRUDEL PASTRY
275 g (10oz) plain flour
pinch of salt
1 teaspoon oil
150 ml (5fl oz) warm water
25 g (1oz) butter, melted
FILLING
25 g (1oz) butter
40 g (1½oz) fresh white breadcrumbs
pinch of ground cinnamon
50 g (2oz) ground almonds
1¼ kg (3lb) cherries
75-100 g (3-4oz) castor sugar
25 g (1oz) melted butter
DECORATION
a little icing sugar

1 **To make the pastry:** Sift the flour and salt into a bowl and make a hollow in the centre. Add the oil and water and mix together, first with a wooden spoon and then with a hand, to form a dough.

2 Knead the dough thoroughly until smooth and elastic, about 5 minutes. Place the dough in a warmed bowl, brush the surface with a little extra oil and cover with polythene. Leave in a warm place for ¾-1 hour.

3 **To make the filling:** Melt the butter in a pan, add the breadcrumbs. Cook, stirring, until the crumbs are golden. Cool.

4 Mix in the cinnamon and ground almonds. Stone the cherries, if liked, and mix in with the sugar.

5 Preheat a moderately hot oven (200 deg C, 400 deg F, Gas 6), centre shelf.

6 **To make the strudel:** Roll out the strudel dough to about 1 cm (½in) thick. Well sprinkle a clean tea towel with flour and lift the dough into the centre. Roll out the dough as thinly as possible with a floured rolling pin, then put both hands under the pastry and pull out the dough to make it as thin as paper.

7 Trim off any thick edges of dough, then brush with melted butter. Spread the prepared filling over about one third of the dough. Then, using the cloth to help, roll the strudel up into a long roll and transfer to a baking sheet – if necessary cut the roll in half.

8 Brush the roll with more melted butter. Bake for about ½ hour until the pastry is crisp and the filling is cooked. Cut into slices.

9 Serve warm, sprinkled with a little icing sugar.

SPICY APPLE CAKES

(Makes 6)
50 g (2oz) butter or margarine
50 g (2oz) castor sugar
1 egg, beaten
125 g (4oz) plain flour, sifted
3 level teaspoons baking powder
½ level teaspoon mixed spice
75 g (3oz) cooking apple, peeled, cored and grated
2 level teaspoons castor sugar for sprinkling

1 Preheat a hot oven (230 deg C, 450 deg F, Gas 8), centre shelf. Grease six 10 cm (4in) round patty tins.

2 Cream the butter and 50 g (2oz) castor sugar, beat in the egg, add the flour, baking powder and spice and fold in with the apple.

3 Put the mixture into the 6 patty tins and sprinkle the tops with castor sugar.

4 Bake for 15 minutes, until browned and firm to touch. Turn out and cool on a wire rack. If liked, sprinkle with extra castor sugar before serving.

BUTTERSCOTCH SQUARES

(Cuts into 9 squares)
125 g (4oz) butterscotch
50 g (2oz) butter
125 g (4oz) soft brown sugar
125 g (4oz) plain flour, sifted
1 level teaspoon baking powder
2 eggs, beaten
50 g (2oz) brazil nuts, chopped
2 teaspoons lemon juice

1 Preheat a moderate oven (180 deg C, 350 deg F, Gas 4), centre shelf. Grease an 18 cm (7in) square tin, and line the base with greased greaseproof paper.

2 Break the butterscotch into pieces, place in a saucepan with the butter. Heat very gently until melted.

3 Remove from the heat, stir in the sugar, add the flour, baking powder, eggs, nuts and lemon juice. Beat well to mix thoroughly.

4 Turn into the cake tin and spread out evenly. Bake for about 25 minutes, until firm to touch.

5 Turn out on to a wire rack, remove greaseproof paper, and leave to cool.

6 Serve cut in squares.

SHERRIED PINEAPPLE CHOCOLATE BOXES

(Makes 24)
125 g (4oz) soft margarine
125 g (4oz) castor sugar
125 g (4oz) self-raising flour
2 large eggs
DECORATION
450 g (1lb) plain dessert chocolate
410 g (14½oz) can pineapple chunks
3 tablespoons sherry
3 tablespoons apricot jam
250 ml (10fl oz) fresh double cream

1 Preheat a moderate oven (180 deg C, 350 deg F, Gas 4), shelf above centre. Grease the base of a Swiss-roll tin 18 cm by 28 cm (7in by 11in) and line with greased greaseproof paper.

2 Combine the soft margarine, sugar, flour and eggs in a mixing bowl and beat well for about 2 minutes until the mixture is light.

3 Spread the creamed mixture in the prepared tin. Bake for about 25 minutes until well risen and firm to the touch. Turn the cake on to a wire rack, remove paper and leave until cold.

4 Meanwhile, break the chocolate in pieces into a bowl and stand it over hot water until the chocolate melts.

5 Spread the melted chocolate on to a sheet of waxed or non-stick paper, or kitchen foil, to a rectangle measuring about 30 cm by 46 cm (12in by 18in) then leave it aside until it has become quite firm.

6 Drain the can of pineapple and reserve the juice. Cut 6 of the larger chunks into 4 and reserve for decoration, then chop the remainder finely. Add the sherry to the pineapple juice.

7 Cut the cake in half through the middle, spread the bottom half with 2 tablespoons of apricot jam, then spoon over the finely chopped pineapple. Place the other layer of cake on top. Prick the cake all over with a fork.

8 Spoon the fruit juice and sherry evenly over the cake and leave it aside until it has soaked in. Cut the soaked cake into 24 squares.

9 Heat the remaining apricot jam with 2 tablespoons water, stir until the jam is thin and then brush it round the sides of the little cakes.

10 Using a very sharp knife, cut the chocolate into 96 squares. Press round the sides of the cakes.

11 Whip the cream until thick and pipe or spoon a little on top of the cakes, decorate each with a piece of pineapple.

CHOCOLATE FUDGE SQUARES

(Cuts into 15 squares)

125 g (4oz) self-raising flour
1 level teaspoon baking powder
2 level tablespoons cocoa
125 g (4oz) soft margarine
125 g (4oz) castor sugar
3 eggs
25 g (1oz) ground almonds
½ teaspoon vanilla essence
ICING
200 g (7oz) icing sugar, sifted
75 g (3oz) soft margarine
2 heaped tablespoons drinking chocolate
1 tablespoon hot water
2 tablespoons milk
icing sugar for sprinkling

1 Preheat a warm oven (170 deg C, 325 deg F, Gas 3), centre shelf. Grease an 18 cm by 28 cm (7in by 11in) rectangular tin and line with greased greaseproof paper.

2 Sift the flour, baking powder and cocoa into a bowl, add the margarine, sugar, eggs, ground almonds and vanilla essence.

3 Beat well for 2-3 minutes until thoroughly well mixed.

4 Place in the prepared tin, level the surface.

5 Cook for 20 minutes until light pressing with the fingertips leaves no mark. Turn out on to a wire rack, remove the paper and allow to cool.

6 To make the icing: Place the icing sugar and margarine in a bowl.

7 Blend the drinking chocolate and hot water together and add with the milk. Beat well together until smooth.

8 Spread the cooled cake with the icing and leave on one side to set.

9 Sprinkle with icing sugar then cut into squares.

COFFEE WALNUT SQUARES

(Cuts into about 15 squares)

150 g (5oz) butter
225 g (8oz) soft brown sugar
175 g (6oz) self-raising flour
25 g (1oz) drinking chocolate
125 g (4oz) walnuts, chopped
3 eggs, beaten
2 level tablespoons instant coffee dissolved in 1 tablespoon boiling water

1 Preheat a warm oven (170 deg C, 325 deg F, Gas 3), centre shelf. Grease a 28 cm by 18 cm (11in by 7in) baking tin and line the base with greased greaseproof paper.

2 Melt the butter and brown sugar in a small saucepan. Allow to cool.

3 Mix the flour, drinking chocolate and walnuts in a mixing bowl and make a well in the centre. Pour in the eggs and dissolved coffee. Mix together while pouring in the melted mixture to make a smooth batter. Beat lightly.

4 Pour into the prepared tin. Bake for 35-40 minutes until risen and just firm to touch. Leave to cool in the tin. Turn out, cut into squares.

SLY CAKES

(Makes about 14)

227 g (8oz) packet frozen puff pastry, thawed
125 g (4oz) currants
50 g (2oz) chopped mixed peel
¼ level teaspoon mixed spice
1 level tablespoon sugar
extra sugar for sprinkling

1 Preheat a hot oven (220 deg C, 425 deg F, Gas 7), shelf above centre. Grease a baking sheet.

2 Roll the thawed pastry out, on a lightly floured surface, into a 30 cm (12in) square, brush with water.

3 Combine the currants, peel, spice and sugar, sprinkle evenly on half of the pastry. Fold the other half over, then roll this until the fruit shows through 'slyly'.

4 Cut into various shapes with a sharp knife and sprinkle with sugar. Transfer to the baking sheet.

5 Bake for 10-15 minutes until risen and golden brown. Cool on a wire rack. Best served the day they are made.

See picture opposite

Sly Cakes, *see opposite*

chapter 6
Biscuits

All kinds of sweet biscuits from the light, thin crisp to the big, crunchy cookie, plus melt-in-the-mouth shortbreads, and flapjacks and oatcakes

CHERRY AND OAT BISCUITS

(Makes 20-24)
75 g (3oz) plain flour
½ level teaspoon bicarbonate of soda
50 g (2oz) glacé cherries, chopped
75 g (3oz) castor sugar
75 g (3oz) rolled oats
100 g (4oz) butter or margarine
1 tablespoon golden syrup
1 tablespoon milk

1 Preheat a cool oven (150 deg C, 300 deg F, Gas 2), shelf above centre. Lightly grease two large baking sheets.
2 Sift together the flour and bicarbonate of soda.
3 Add the cherries to the flour with the sugar and rolled oats and mix together.
4 Melt the butter and golden syrup in a small saucepan, stir in the milk.
5 Stir the liquid ingredients into the dry ingredients until thoroughly combined. Cool for 5 minutes in the fridge.
6 Take heaped teaspoonsful of the mixture and roll into balls. Place well apart on the baking sheets. Flatten on top with a fork.
7 Bake for 20-25 minutes or until lightly browned.
8 Cool in tin for a few minutes. Finish cooling on rack.

GINGERNUTS

(Makes about 24)
50 g (2oz) butter
50 g (2oz) soft brown sugar
50 g (2oz) golden syrup
50 g (2oz) black treacle
175 g (6oz) self-raising flour
1 level teaspoon ground ginger

1 Preheat a moderate oven (180 deg C, 350 deg F, Gas 4), centre shelf. Lightly grease two baking sheets.
2 Heat the butter gently in a saucepan, add sugar, syrup and treacle. Stir until dissolved, do not get too hot.
3 Sift the flour and ginger and add to the pan. Then mix to firm paste.
4 Take rounded teaspoonsful and place on a baking sheet leaving space for biscuits to spread.
5 Cook for 15 minutes, one sheet at a time. Remove from oven and press the tops with a fork. Leave on the baking sheet for a few seconds then cool on a wire rack.
6 Repeat until all the mixture is used up.

See picture on page 15

*It is important to follow **either** the metric **or** the imperial weights and measures in any one recipe*

CURLY COFFEE BISCUITS

(Makes about 24)
2 egg whites
100 g (4oz) castor sugar
1 rounded teaspoon instant coffee powder
1 teaspoon boiling water
50 g (2oz) butter, melted
50 g (2oz) plain flour, sifted

1 Preheat a moderately hot oven (190 deg C, 375 deg F, Gas 5), shelf above centre. Well-grease two baking sheets.
2 Whisk the egg whites till stiff, gradually whisk in the castor sugar.
3 Dissolve the instant coffee in the boiling water.
4 Carefully fold the coffee and butter into the meringue, with the flour.
5 Place small teaspoonsful of the mixture on to the baking sheets, spaced well apart, placing no more than 6 on each sheet, for easy handling.
6 Bake for 7-8 minutes, until the edges are browned. Quickly and carefully, using a palette knife, lift each biscuit off the baking sheet and press on to a rolling pin to curl. Cool the biscuits on a wire rack.
7 Continue in this way until all the mixture is used up.
Note: *The biscuits should be stored in an airtight tin as soon as they have cooled, or they will uncurl.*

VIENNESE CRUNCHY CREAMS

(Makes 15)
100 g (4oz) butter or soft margarine
50 g (2oz) castor sugar
100 g (4oz) self-raising flour
1 level tablespoon cornflour
¼ level teaspoon baking powder
1 level tablespoon instant coffee powder
25 g (1oz) chopped dessert chocolate or chocolate drops
  for cooking
CHOCOLATE BUTTER ICING
75 g (3oz) icing sugar
1 level tablespoon cocoa
40 g (1½oz) butter or margarine
1 teaspoon hot water

1 Preheat a moderately hot oven (200 deg C, 400 deg F, Gas 6), shelves above and below centre. Grease two baking sheets.
2 Cream the butter with the sugar until light and fluffy.
3 Sift the flour, cornflour, baking powder and instant coffee together and fold them into the creamed mixture with the chopped chocolate or chocolate drops.
4 Place teaspoonsful (about 30) of the mixture on the baking sheets. Bake for about 10 minutes, changing the tins around to ensure even cooking.
5 Cool for a few minutes on the baking sheets, then transfer the biscuits to a wire rack to cool.
6 **To make the chocolate butter icing:** Sift the icing sugar

and cocoa. Then cream the butter until light and fluffy, and gradually beat in the sugar mixture and the teaspoon of hot water.
7 Sandwich the biscuits together in pairs with the chocolate butter icing.
8 Sprinkle with icing sugar to serve.

HONEY CRUNCH BISCUITS

(Makes 24)
100 g (4oz) butter
50 g (2oz) castor sugar
grated rind 1 lemon
2 level tablespoons thick honey
1 egg yolk
175 g (6oz) self-raising flour
24 split almonds

1 Preheat a moderate oven (180 deg C, 350 deg F, Gas 4), shelf above centre. Grease two baking sheets.
2 Cream the butter with the sugar, lemon rind and honey until fluffy, then beat in the egg yolk.
3 Sift in the flour and mix to make a stiff dough. Form the mixture into 24 balls, place on the baking sheets.
4 Flatten each ball slightly and place an almond in the centre.
5 Bake for 12-15 minutes until light brown. Cool on a wire rack.

TREACLE OAT CURLS

(Makes 30)
75 g (3oz) butter or margarine
75 g (3oz) castor sugar
75 g (3oz) demerara sugar
2 level tablespoons black treacle
1 level tablespoon golden syryp
1 level teaspoon bicarbonate of soda
1 tablespoon hot water
50 g (2oz) rolled oats
75 g (3oz) fine or medium oatmeal
50 g (2oz) plain flour
rolled oats for decoration

1 Preheat a warm oven (170 deg C, 325 deg F, Gas 3), centre shelf. Grease at least two baking sheets. Oil two rolling pins or narrow bottles.
2 Heat the butter, sugars, treacle and syrup until the sugar has melted. Dissolve the bicarbonate of soda in the water and mix into pan. Remove from heat.
3 Mix the oats, oatmeal and flour in a bowl. Pour in the melted mixture and mix thoroughly. Place about 6 small teaspoonsful of the mixture on a baking sheet, well spaced apart to allow for spreading. Flatten slightly and sprinkle each with a pinch of oats.
4 Bake, a sheet at a time, for about 10 minutes until brown and bubbling. Cool slightly on the sheet but lift off carefully while still hot, using a palette knife. Then

mould round rolling pins or bottles for a curled shape.
5 Cook rest of mixture in the same way. Remove the biscuits from the rolling pins when cool. Repeat for the next batch.

See picture opposite, bottom left of jar

BRAZILIAN NUGGETS

(Makes 24)
225 g (8oz) plain flour
125 g (4oz) butter or margarine
125 g (4oz) soft brown sugar
50 g (2oz) brazil nuts, coarsely chopped
1 level tablespoon instant coffee
2 teaspoons hot water
1 egg, beaten

1 Preheat a moderate oven (180 deg C, 350 deg F, Gas 4), shelves above and below centre. Grease two baking sheets.
2 Put the flour in a bowl, cut in the butter and rub in. Mix in the sugar and nuts.
3 Dissolve the coffee in the water. Make a well in the dry ingredients, add the coffee and egg, mix to a stiff dough. Form into walnut-sized pieces and place on the baking sheets. Flatten with a fork.
4 Bake for 20-25 minutes until lightly coloured, changing the shelf positions after 10 minutes. Cool on a wire rack.

See picture opposite, foreground

HAZELNUT MACAROONS

(Makes 10)
1 egg white
75 g (3oz) castor sugar
50 g (2oz) hazelnuts, finely chopped
2-3 drops almond essence
10 whole hazelnuts

1 Preheat a moderate oven (180 deg C, 350 deg F, Gas 4), centre shelf. Line a baking sheet with non-stick paper.
2 Whisk the egg white and sugar in a bowl over hot water until white and thick enough to hold the trail of the whisk when it is lifted.
3 Remove from heat. Fold in the chopped hazelnuts and almond essence.
4 Place dessertspoonsful of the mixture on the baking sheet. Put a whole hazelnut on top of each.
5 Bake for 15-20 minutes until lightly brown and crisp. Cool on a wire rack.

See picture opposite, bottom right of jar

ROUNDABOUTS

(Makes about 22)
125 g (4oz) butter or margarine
125 g (4oz) castor sugar
1 egg yolk
225 g (8oz) plain flour
ICING
225 g (8oz) icing sugar, sifted
a little lemon juice (optional)
food colouring (optional)
DECORATION
sugar strands, 'hundreds and thousands'
   or chocolate vermicelli

1 Preheat a moderate oven (180 deg C, 350 deg F, Gas 4), shelves above and below centre. Grease two baking sheets.
2 Cream the butter and castor sugar until soft and fluffy. Beat in the egg yolk, then work in the flour until the mixture forms a ball.
3 Roll out on a lightly floured surface to $\frac{1}{2}$ cm ($\frac{1}{4}$in) thick. Cut out rings, using a 6 cm (2$\frac{1}{2}$in) doughnut cutter (or two sizes of biscuit cutter).
4 Bake 10 minutes, change position of baking sheets and cook for a further 10 minutes until lightly coloured. Cool a minute, then lift on to wire racks. Cool.
5 **To make the icing:** Mix the icing sugar with just enough lemon juice or hot water to make a thick icing. Colour lightly if liked. Spread on the biscuits and sprinkle with decorations. Leave to set.

See picture opposite, top right

CHOCOLATE CHIPPIES

(Makes about 20)
125 g (4oz) butter
75 g (3oz) castor sugar
1 egg yolk
150 g (5oz) self-raising flour
50 g (2oz) chocolate drops for cooking
about 25 g (1oz) dessicated
   coconut (optional)

1 Preheat a moderately hot oven (190 deg C, 375 deg F, Gas 5), towards top and centre shelves. Lightly grease two baking sheets.
2 Cream the butter and sugar until soft. Beat in the egg yolk. Stir in the flour and chocolate drops until well mixed.
3 Form into about 20 small walnut-sized balls, rolling the mixture between the hands. If liked, roll in coconut. Place on the baking sheets, allowing room for spreading.
4 Bake for 15-20 minutes until lightly browned. Cool on the sheets for one minute, then lift on to a wire rack and leave to finish cooling.

In jar: **Hazelnut Macaroons** *and* **Roundabouts,** *see opposite;* **Orange Bars,** *page 57;* **Ginger Crispies,** *page 89;* **Cinnamon Twists** *and*
Sweet Susie Puffs, *below;* **Treacle Oat Curls,** *page 53. In front:* **Brazilian Nuggets,** *opposite*

SWEET SUSIE PUFFS

(Makes 12)
50 g (2oz) butter or margarine
150 ml (5fl oz) water
75 g (3oz) plain flour
25 g (1oz) castor sugar
2 eggs, beaten
½ teaspoon vanilla essence
oil for deep frying
castor or icing sugar for serving

1 Melt the butter in the water. Bring to the boil, remove from heat, add the flour and sugar all at once. Beat rapidly until the mixture binds and leaves the sides of the saucepan cleanly. Leave to cool for about 5 minutes.
2 Gradually beat in the eggs a little at a time, and the vanilla essence, until smooth and glossy.
3 Heat the oil until a cube of bread fried in it turns golden brown in 30 seconds. Drop in 6 small dessertspoonsful of puff mixture and fry for 4-5 minutes, turning once, until puffy, brown and cooked. Lift one out and drain on kitchen paper. (If a puff collapses slightly, it is not cooked

through, so return to pan.)
4 Fry remaining mixture in the same way. Toss in castor or icing sugar while hot, or cool and sprinkle with icing sugar. Best eaten very fresh, and preferably still warm.
See picture above, top centre

CINNAMON TWISTS

(Makes 12)
50 g (2oz) castor sugar
1 level teaspoon ground cinnamon
212 g (7½oz) packet frozen puff pastry, thawed

1 Preheat a hot oven (220 deg C, 425 deg F, Gas 7), shelf above centre. Lightly damp a baking sheet.
2 Mix the sugar and cinnamon and sprinkle half on to a work surface.
3 Roll out the pastry on the sugar mixture, sprinkling the rest on top and rolling it in. Roll to a 25 cm (10in) square.
4 Cut into 12 equal strips, damp one end of each and twist to form a spiral. Press the ends together to seal, arrange 6 twists on the baking sheet.

55

5 Bake for 10 minutes, turn the twists over and cook a further 5 minutes until they are brown and crisp and the sugar has caramelised. Cool on a wire rack. Clean the baking sheet and cook the remaining twists in the same way. These will keep for one day in an airtight container.

See picture on page 55, left

OATCAKES

(Makes 32)
450 g (1lb) porridge oats
½ level teaspoon bicarbonate of soda
pinch of salt
25 g (1oz) lard
275 ml (½ pint) hot water

1 Preheat a moderately hot oven (190 deg C, 375 deg F, Gas 5), centre shelf. Lightly flour two baking sheets.
2 Place the oats, bicarbonate of soda and salt in a bowl. Mix well, make a hollow in the centre.
3 Melt the lard in the hot water and pour into the hollow, mix with a knife until a soft dough.
4 Sprinkle surface with oats or wholemeal flour and roll out the dough to 6 mm (¼in) thick, then cut out four 15 cm (6in) rounds. Mark each in four.
5 Place on the baking sheets, re-roll trimmings and cut remainder into 6 cm (2¼in) rounds. Fit on to the sheets.
6 Cook in two batches for 20 minutes, turning the biscuits after 10 minutes. Cool on a wire rack.

HONEY AND HAZELNUT BISCUITS

(Makes 20-24)
125 g (4oz) butter
250 g (8oz) castor sugar
1 egg
1 teaspoon vanilla essence
250 g (8oz) plain flour
¼ teaspoon salt
2 level teaspoons baking powder
FILLING AND TOPPING
4 tablespoons thick honey
100 g (4oz) hazelnuts, skinned and finely chopped
75 g (3oz) plain chocolate

1 Beat the butter until soft, add the sugar and cream well until light and fluffy.
2 Add the egg and beat until the mixture is thick. Stir in the vanilla essence.
3 Sift the flour, salt and baking powder together, then fold into the mixture. Chill if necessary then shape into a roll about 4 cm (1½in) in diameter. Wrap in cling film and chill until firm.
4 Preheat a moderately hot oven (200 deg C, 400 deg F, Gas 6), centre shelf. Grease two baking sheets.
5 Cut dough into 40-48 thin slices. Place on sheets.
6 Bake in two batches for about 10 minutes until lightly brown. Lift straight on to a wire rack to cool. When cold,

---

store in an airtight container until required.
7 To make the filling and topping: Combine the honey and hazelnuts, sandwich biscuits together in pairs.
8 Break the chocolate in pieces and melt in a small basin standing over a pan of hot water. Dip in one edge of each sandwiched biscuit and place on a wire rack until set.

ORANGE HEARTS

(Makes 24)
100 g (4oz) butter or margarine
100 g (4oz) castor sugar
1 egg
grated rind 1 orange
225 g (8oz) plain flour
50 g (2oz) mixed peel, finely chopped

1 Preheat a moderate oven (180 deg C, 350 deg F, Gas 4), centre shelf. Grease two baking sheets.
2 Cream the butter with the sugar until light and fluffy. Beat in the egg and orange rind.
3 Sift in the flour and add the peel using fingertips, work the mixture to form a soft but not sticky dough.
4 Knead the dough lightly, then roll out on a lightly floured surface to about 6 mm (¼in) thick. Cut out into 7.5 cm (3in) heart shapes, rounds or stars.
5 Place on baking sheets. Bake one at a time for 15-20 minutes until lightly coloured. Cool on a wire rack.

SPICY REFRIGERATOR BISCUITS

(Makes about 25-30)
100 g (4oz) butter, softened
100 g (4oz) soft brown sugar
50 g (2oz) golden syrup
1 level teaspoon cream of tartar
1 teaspoon water
25 g (1oz) chopped almonds
25 g (1oz) chopped mixed peel
225 g (8oz) plain flour
½ level teaspoon ground nutmeg
½ level teaspoon ground cinnamon
½ level teaspoon ground cloves

1 Cream the butter and sugar until soft, beat in syrup.
2 Blend the cream of tartar with the water and add with the almonds and peel.
3 Sift the flour and spices together, work into mixture.
4 Shape into a roll about 5 cm (2in) in diameter. Wrap in foil, place in refrigerator for about one hour, until firm.
5 Preheat a moderate oven (190 deg C, 375 deg F, Gas 5), shelf above centre. Grease a baking sheet.
6 Cut the chilled roll into thin slices about 6 mm (¼in) thick. Place on the baking sheet and cook for about 7 minutes until lightly browned.
7 Cool for a few seconds on sheet, then on wire rack.

Note: *The uncooked mixture can be kept in the refrigerator for up to 2 weeks.*

CHERRY WHIRLS

(Makes 8)
125 g (4oz) butter or margarine
50 g (2oz) icing sugar
1 egg yolk
150 g (5oz) plain flour
25 g (1oz) cornflour
pink food colouring
50 g (2oz) glacé cherries
BUTTER ICING
50 g (2oz) butter or margarine, softened
125 g (4oz) icing sugar, sifted
2 teaspoons lemon juice

1 Cream the butter and icing sugar until soft and fluffy, then beat in the egg yolk. Sift the flour and cornflour and mix into the mixture. Halve the mixture and knead a little colouring into one half until evenly pink.
2 Using a large piping bag with a large star tube, pipe first the plain mixture into 8 rosettes on to a greased baking sheet and then the coloured mixture. Cut up a few of the cherries to make 16 pieces and put a piece on each rosette. Chill one hour.
3 Preheat a moderately hot oven (190 deg C, 375 deg F, Gas 5), centre shelf.
4 Bake for about 15 minutes until beginning to colour lightly. Cool one minute, lift on to a wire rack to finish cooling.
5 **To make the butter icing:** Cream the butter, gradually beat in the icing sugar and lemon juice to make a smooth icing. Chop remaining cherries and mix in. Use to sandwich the biscuits, putting a pink and cream half together.

DARK GINGER FLAPJACK

(Cuts into about 24 pieces)
175 g (6oz) butter or margarine
175 g (6oz) golden syrup
125 g (4 oz) black treacle
125 g (4oz) dark brown sugar
350 g (12oz) rolled oats
75 g (3oz) oatmeal
2 level teaspoons ground ginger

1 Preheat a moderate oven (180 deg C, 350 deg F, Gas 4), centre shelf. Grease a Swiss-roll tin about 23 cm by 33 cm (9in by 13in).
2 Heat the butter or margarine, syrup, treacle and sugar in a saucepan until melted. Stir in the oats, oatmeal and ginger. Remove from heat. Mix very well.
3 Turn into the prepared tin and level the surface. Bake for 25-30 minutes. (The shorter baking time gives a soft, sticky result, and the longer baking time gives a harder, crisp result.) Cut into pieces while still hot, leave 10 minutes then ease out on to a wire rack to cool. Keeps well in an airtight container for up to 10 days.

OAT CRUNCH

(Cuts into 12 pieces)
125 g (4oz) butter or margarine
75 g (3oz) soft brown sugar
grated rind 1 orange
50 g (2oz) walnuts
175 g (6oz) rolled oats

1 Preheat a moderately hot oven (190 deg C, 375 deg F, Gas 5), shelf above centre. Grease a shallow oblong tin about 28 cm by 18 cm (11in by 7in) using lightly buttered paper.
2 Cream the butter and sugar until light and puffy.
3 Beat in the grated orange rind and stir in the walnuts and rolled oats.
4 Press the mixture into the prepared tin and level the surface. Bake for 25 minutes until the top is pale golden brown.
5 Mark into 12 pieces while still hot and leave to cool in the tin.
6 Cut the pieces right through, then lift out and store in an airtight tin.

ORANGE BARS

(Makes 12)
175 g (6oz) plain flour
50 g (2oz) semolina
75 g (3oz) castor sugar
175 g (6oz) butter or margarine
finely grated rind 1 orange
TOPPING
175 g (6oz) icing sugar
orange juice

1 Preheat a warm oven (170 deg C, 325 deg F, Gas 3), centre shelf. Grease a shallow 18 cm (7in) square tin.
2 Mix the flour, semolina and castor sugar together in a bowl. Add the butter and rub in finely. Mix in the orange rind. Turn into the tin, press down.
3 Bake for 45 minutes until firm.
4 **To make the topping:** Meanwhile mix the icing sugar with sufficient orange juice to make a thick coating consistency. Spread over the hot biscuit and return to the oven for 10 minutes.
5 Cool in the tin 10 minutes. Mark into 12 bars, then lift on to a wire rack to cool.

See picture on page 55, right

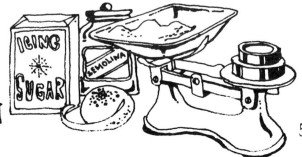

BUTTERY-CRISP BISCUITS

(Makes about 30)
225 g (8oz) butter
275 g (10oz) plain flour
125 g (4oz) icing sugar
½ teaspoon vanilla essence

1 Knead all the ingredients together with the fingertips in a mixing bowl to make a firm dough.
2 Wrap in foil or greaseproof paper and leave mixture to chill for 20 minutes in a cool place.
3 Meanwhile preheat a moderately hot oven (200 deg C, 400 deg F, Gas 6), shelf above centre. Grease a baking sheet.
4 Roll out the dough on a lightly floured surface until it is 3 mm (⅛in) thick.
5 Using a 6 cm (2¼in) fluted cutter, stamp out rounds and place on the baking sheet. Prick well with a fork.
6 Bake for 8-10 minutes. Cool for a moment on the baking sheet then lift carefully on to a wire rack to finish cooling.
7 Serve plain, or iced with glacé or butter icing. Biscuits may be sandwiched together with jam, and if liked, sprinkled with sifted icing sugar.

See picture opposite, above

TREACLE AND RAISIN FLAPJACKS

(Makes 9-12 pieces)
75 g (3oz) butter or margarine
125 g (4oz) golden syrup
1 slightly rounded tablespoon black treacle
25 g (1oz) brown sugar
50 g (2oz) seedless raisins
125 g (4oz) rolled oats

1 Preheat a moderate oven (180 deg C, 350 deg F, Gas 4), centre shelf. Oil a 20 cm (8in) square tin.
2 Place the butter in a saucepan and add the syrup, treacle and brown sugar.
3 Heat gently until melted, then stir in the raisins and rolled oats. Stir until evenly mixed.
4 Turn into the tin and spread out using the back of a spoon. Bake for 20-25 minutes until lightly coloured.
5 Cut into 9-12 pieces while still hot, leave 10 minutes then ease out on to a wire rack to cool. It will keep in an airtight container for up to 10 days.

See picture opposite, below

SHORTBREAD FINGERS

(Makes 12)
125 g (5oz) plain flour
25 g (1oz) rice flour
50 g (2oz) castor sugar
100 g (4oz) butter
extra castor sugar (optional)

1 Preheat a warm oven (170 deg C, 325 deg F, Gas 3), shelf just above centre. Grease an 18 cm (7in) square sandwich tin.
2 Sift the flours and sugar into a bowl. Knead the butter into the mixture until it binds.
3 Turn into the tin, level the surface. Prick well with fork.
4 Bake 40-45 minutes until lightly brown. Mark into 12 fingers and leave in the tin for 5 minutes.
5 Cool on a wire rack. Dredge with sugar, if liked.

See picture opposite, below

REFRIGERATOR HARLEQUINS

(Makes about 18)
125 g (4oz) butter
75 g (3oz) castor sugar
150 g (5oz) plain flour
4 drops vanilla essence
1 rounded teaspoon cocoa
3 drops almond essence
green and pink food colouring
'hundreds and thousands'

1 Cream the butter and sugar until soft and pale. Work in the flour until well mixed. Divide into 4 even pieces.
2 Knead the vanilla essence into one piece of dough, the cocoa into another piece, the almond essence and several drops green colouring into the third piece of dough, several drops pink colouring into the last piece.
3 Roll each piece of dough into a 15 cm (6in) roll.
4 Place the rolls together and then press and roll gently together to make one 15 cm (6in) roll. Roll in 'hundreds and thousands', pressing down gently to coat. Wrap in waxed paper. Chill.
5 Preheat a moderately hot oven (190 deg C, 375 deg F, Gas 5), centre shelf. Lightly grease two baking sheets.
6 Cut the biscuit dough in thin slices and place on the baking sheets, bake one sheet at a time for 8-10 minutes until lightly coloured. Lift on to a wire rack to cool.

Note: *The uncooked mixture can be kept in a refrigerator for up to 2 weeks.*

Top: **Buttery-Crisp Biscuits,** *see opposite. Above:* **Shortbread Fingers** *and* **Treacle and Raisin Flapjacks,** *see opposite*

chapter 7
Yeast Bakes

Home-made bread at its best, and the special yeasty
loaves and buns and pastries that make a really
memorable tea

Note: If using dried yeast which you have had in store for
some time, test for freshness by putting in warm water
with a little sugar and leaving for 20 minutes. If still
active, it should develop a bubbling froth of about 1.5 cm
(½in) depth.

WHOLEMEAL BREAD

*(Use to make battens, cobs, tins and flower pot loaves. Makes 4
loaves: 1 of each shape or 4 the same)*

2 level teaspoons castor sugar
900 ml (1 pint 13fl oz) tepid water
20 g (¾oz) sachet dried yeast
2 tablespoons black treacle
1.5 kg (3.31 lb) bag plain wholemeal flour
1 level tablespoon salt
125 g (4oz) margarine

1 Stir the sugar into 150 ml (5fl oz) of the measured water,
sprinkle the dried yeast on top and stir. Leave in a warm
place for 10-20 minutes until the yeast becomes frothy.
2 Meanwhile, dissolve the treacle in the rest of the
measured water.
3 Sift the flour and salt into a very large mixing bowl. Rub
in the margarine. Make a well in the centre and pour in
the yeast liquid and the treacle liquid. Mix to form a
dough.
4 Knead the dough on a floured surface for about 10
minutes until smooth and elastic. Put into a lightly oiled
polythene bag, close the bag and put in a warm (not hot)
place until the dough rises to double its size. (This will
take 1-1½ hours, depending on room temperature.)

5 Meanwhile, decide which shaped loaves to make and
well-grease the tins or pots to be used: for batten or cob, a
baking sheet; for tin, a small loaf tin; for pot, a 15 cm (6in)
proved flower pot (see note at top of next page).
6 Turn the risen dough on to a floured surface, knock
back to its original size by beating hard with clenched
fists. Knead again for 5 minutes. Cut the dough into 4
pieces and return 3 pieces to the oiled polythene bag
while shaping the first.
7 To shape:
Batten: Roll one piece of dough into a 30 cm (12in) long,
tapered (cigar-shaped) roll. Place on a baking sheet, and
make 5 or 6 deep, diagonal cuts into loaf.
Cob: Shape into a neat ball, then press out into a round 19
cm (7½in) in diameter. Place on a baking sheet.
Tin: Knead and shape into an oblong and press into a
loaf tin.
Flower pot loaf: Knead and form into a ball and press into
a flower pot.
8 Cover the loaves with oiled polythene bags and put in a
warm place to rise. (If your oven is not large enough to
take all the loaves at once, the proving process may be
slowed down by putting some of the loaves in the
refrigerator.) Leave the loaves in a warm (not hot) place
until they have doubled in size, and the dough springs
back easily when pressed with a floured finger. (This will
take 20-30 minutes depending on the temperature in the
kitchen.)
9 Meanwhile, preheat a hot oven (230 deg C, 450 deg F,
Gas 8), shelves above and below centre.
10 Before baking the loaves, sprinkle the cob and batten
with a little extra flour. Mix one teaspoon salt with a little
cold water and use to brush the tops of the tin and flower
pot loaves.
11 Bake the loaves for 30-40 minutes, until they are well
risen, golden brown, and sound hollow when tapped on
the bases. Cool on a wire rack. Eat within one day of

*It is important to follow **either** the metric **or** the imperial weights
and measures in any one recipe*

making. But stale loaves are always ideal for toasting.

Proving flower pots

Before using flower pots for baking they should be proved. To do this, select a new clay (not plastic) flower pot, scrub well in hot soapy water, rinse and dry thoroughly. When the pot is completely dry, brush it well inside and outside with melted lard. Place the pot on a baking sheet and put in a warm oven (170 deg C, 325 deg F, Gas 3) until the lard is absorbed and the pot looks dry, then brush with more melted lard and repeat the process. Keep repeating until the pot becomes very smooth and shiny, and will not absorb any more lard.

QUICKLY-MADE WHITE BREAD

(Use to make cottage loaves, bumpy loaves and dinner rolls. Makes 1 large and 1 small loaf and 12 rolls, or 2 large loaves, or 1 large loaf and 24 rolls)

2 level teaspoons castor sugar
900 ml (1 pint 13fl oz) tepid water
20 g (¾oz) sachet dried yeast
50 mg ascorbic acid (Vitamin C) tablet
1.5 kg (3.31 lb) bag strong plain white flour
1 level tablespoon salt
25 g (1oz) margarine
1 egg, beaten, for glazing
poppy seeds (optional)

1 Stir the sugar into 150 ml (5fl oz) of the measured water, sprinkle the yeast on top and stir. Leave to stand in a warm place until frothy, about 10-20 minutes.
2 Dissolve the ascorbic acid tablet in the remaining measured water, stir in the yeast liquid.
3 Sift the flour and salt into a very large mixing bowl and rub in the margarine. Make a well in the centre, pour in the yeast liquid and mix to form a dough.
4 Turn the dough on to a floured surface and knead well for about 10 minutes until smooth and elastic. Return the dough to a clean mixing bowl, cover with oiled polythene and leave in a warm (not hot) place for 10 minutes.
5 Grease two baking sheets and an 825 ml (1½ pint) loaf tin if making one cottage and one bumpy loaf and rolls.
6 Turn the dough on to a floured surface and knead once again for 5 minutes. Divide the dough in two and then wrap one piece of dough in polythene.
7 To shape:
Cottage loaf: Take the unwrapped dough (keep the other piece covered) and cut off one third. Knead both pieces until smooth and shape into neat rounds. Place the largest piece on a baking sheet, then place the small piece directly on top. Flour the handle of a wooden spoon and insert it through the centre of both pieces of dough, then remove it. Cover with a lightly oiled polythene bag.
Rolls: Cut remaining dough in half. Cut one half into 12 pieces. Knead and shape these into neat rounds. Place on a baking sheet.
Bumpy loaf: Cut the last piece of dough into 4 equal pieces, knead and shape into neat rounds – place these side by side in the loaf tin. Cover the rolls and loaf with lightly oiled polythene bags.

8 Leave the loaves and rolls in a warm place to rise. This will take 30-45 minutes, depending on the temperature of your kitchen. The rolls will take a little less time.
9 Meanwhile, preheat a hot oven (230 deg C, 450 deg F, Gas 8), shelves above and below centre.
10 When the loaves have doubled in size, and the dough springs back when pressed with a floured finger, brush the loaves and rolls with egg, sprinkle the rolls with poppy seeds, if liked. Bake until they are well risen, golden brown, and sound hollow when tapped on the bases. Cottage loaf will take 45-50 minutes, bumpy loaf will take 25-30 minutes and rolls 15-20 minutes. Cool on a wire rack. Eat within one day of making. Stale loaves are ideal for toasting.

CHEESE AND ONION CROWN

(Makes 6 rolls)

15 g (½oz) fresh yeast
200 ml (7fl oz) water
350 g (12oz) strong plain white flour
½ level teaspoon salt
½ level teaspoon sugar
15 g (½oz) lard
75 g (3oz) grated Cheddar cheese
1 small onion, grated

1 Blend the yeast and water and place on one side until frothy (about 10-20 minutes).
2 Put the flour, salt and sugar in a bowl and rub in the lard. Add 50 g (2oz) of the cheese and all the onion.
3 Mix in the yeast liquid, using a wooden fork or spoon. Work to a firm dough until the sides of the bowl are clean.
4 Turn on to a lightly floured surface and knead thoroughly until smooth and elastic, about 10 minutes. Place in an oiled polythene bag, put in a warm place until double in size (about 40-60 minutes).
5 Turn the dough out and knead for a few minutes. Cut into 6 pieces, place in a greased 18 cm (7in) sandwich tin, with one roll in the centre. Sprinkle with the remaining cheese.
6 Cover with a lightly oiled polythene bag and put in a warm place until the rolls have doubled in size (about 20 minutes).
7 Meanwhile, preheat a moderately hot oven (200 deg C, 400 deg F, Gas 6), centre shelf.
8 Remove from the bag. Bake for 20-25 minutes until the crown is golden and sounds hollow when tapped on the base. Turn out on a wire rack to cool.
9 Serve sliced and buttered.

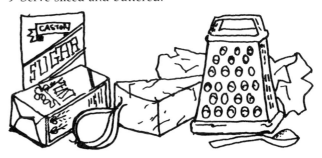

FRUITY LOAF

(Cuts into about 15 slices)
1 level teaspoon castor sugar
225 ml (8fl oz) tepid milk
2 level teaspoons dried yeast
450 g (1lb) plain flour
1 level teaspoon salt
15 g (½oz) butter
175 g (6oz) mixed dried fruit
1 egg, beaten
TOPPING
1 level tablespoon thick honey
25 g (1oz) glacé cherries, quartered
25 g (1oz) blanched almonds, roughly chopped

1 Dissolve the sugar in the milk, sprinkle the yeast on top. Leave in a warm place until frothy, about 20 minutes.
2 Place the flour and salt in a bowl. Rub in the butter. Stir in the fruit and make a hollow in the centre.
3 Add the egg to the yeast mixture, pour into the hollow. Mix to a soft dough. Knead on a floured surface until smooth and no longer sticky, for about 10 minutes.
4 Place the dough in an oiled polythene bag. Put in a warm place until double in size (1½-2 hours).
5 Well-grease a 1½-litre (2½-pint) loaf tin.
6 Turn the dough on to a floured surface, knead until smooth, shape and place in the tin. Cover with oiled polythene, put in a warm place until the dough rises to the top of the tin (about ½ hour).
7 Preheat a moderately hot oven (200 deg C, 400 deg F, Gas 6), centre shelf.
8 Bake 40-45 minutes until the loaf sounds hollow when tapped on the base. Turn out and cool on a wire rack.
9 **To make the topping:** Place the honey in a small saucepan and boil for one minute. Stir in the cherries and nuts and spread over the top of the loaf. Leave to set.
10 Serve cut in slices, spread with butter, if liked.

QUICK YORKSHIRE TEACAKES

(Makes 6)
25 g (1oz) fresh yeast
275 ml (½ pint) warm milk
25 mg ascorbic acid (Vitamin C) tablet
450 g (1lb) strong plain white flour
1 level teaspoon salt
25 g (1oz) sugar
25 g (1oz) lard
75 g (3oz) currants
milk to brush

1 Blend the yeast and milk, add the ascorbic acid tablet and stir to dissolve. Leave to stand in a warm place until frothy (10-20 minutes).
2 Put the flour, salt and sugar in a large bowl, rub in the lard. Add the fruit.
3 Mix the yeast liquid with the dry ingredients using a wooden fork or spoon. Work to a firm dough, adding extra flour if necessary until sides of bowl are clean.
4 Turn the dough on to a lightly floured surface and knead thoroughly until smooth and elastic (5-10 minutes). To do this, fold the dough towards you and then push down and away with the heel of the hand.
5 Shape the dough into a ball, place in a lightly oiled polythene bag and leave to stand for 10 minutes.
6 Knock back the dough and divide into 6 equal pieces.
7 Form into rounds and roll each round out to a diameter of 10-13 cm (4-5in).
8 Place well apart on lightly greased baking sheets and cover with oiled polythene. Allow to rise in a warm place until almost double in size (this takes about 30 minutes).
9 Meanwhile, preheat a moderately hot oven (200 deg C, 400 deg F, Gas 6), shelves above and below centre.
10 Brush dough with milk, bake 15-20 minutes, until teacakes are golden brown and hollow when tapped on bases. Serve warm or toasted, with butter.

Note: *If 25 mg ascorbic acid tablets are not available, use half a 50 mg tablet.*

See picture opposite

FLUFFY JAM DOUGHNUTS

(Makes about 6)
BATTER
50 g (2oz) plain flour
½ level teaspoon sugar
15 g (½oz) fresh yeast, or 2 level teaspoons dried yeast
100 ml (4fl oz) warm milk
DOUGH
175 g (6oz) plain flour
½ level teaspoon salt
15 g (½oz) butter, margarine or lard
1 egg, beaten
oil or fat for deep frying
jam for filling
COATING
50 g (2oz) castor sugar
½ level teaspoon cinnamon

1 Blend the batter ingredients together in a large bowl and set aside until the batter froths (20-30 minutes).
2 Add the dough ingredients and mix to give a fairly soft dough that leaves the side of the bowl clean.
3 Turn the dough on to a lightly floured surface and knead until it is smooth, elastic and no longer sticky (about 10 minutes). Put to rise in a lightly greased polythene bag, loosely tied, until double in size (1-1½ hours at room temperature, longer in a refrigerator).
4 Knead the dough thoroughly, cut into 6 rounds, place on an oiled baking sheet. Cover with oiled polythene.
5 Leave to rise until the rounds have again doubled in size (20-30 minutes). Heat oil or fat for deep frying.
6 Place a small quantity of stiff jam in the centres of the risen doughnuts and pinch into shape.
7 Deep fry for 4 minutes at 185 deg C (360 deg F) – the fat should be hot enough to brown bread in one minute – turning doughnuts carefully over with a slotted spoon.
8 Drain and roll in mixed sugar and cinnamon.

Quick Yorkshire Teacakes, *see opposite*

GUERNSEY GACHE

(Cuts into 10-12 slices)

25 g (1oz) fresh yeast
1 level tablespoon castor sugar
150 ml (5fl oz) warm water
225 g (8oz) margarine
350 g (12oz) plain flour
225 g (8oz) currants
50 g (2oz) chopped mixed peel
25 g (1oz) castor sugar
½ level teaspoon salt
½ level teaspoon freshly grated nutmeg

1 Cream the yeast and one tablespoon of sugar, blend in the water. Leave until frothy (10-20 minutes).
2 Rub the margarine into the flour, add remaining ingredients, stir the yeast liquid and add.
3 Mix with a wooden fork or spoon then turn on to a floured surface and knead until smooth and elastic (5-10 minutes) – this is quite a soft mixture.
4 Shape into an oblong. Lightly oil a 1½-litre (2½-pint) loaf tin.
5 Place the dough in the tin, level the surface with the knuckles, cover with a lightly oiled polythene bag, leave in a warm place until the mixture reaches the top of the tin (about ½ hour).
6 Bake in a moderately hot oven (200 deg C, 400 deg F, Gas 6), centre shelf, for about one hour, until brown and sounds hollow when rapped with the knuckles.

SALLY LUNN

(Cuts into 10 slices)

15 g (½oz) fresh yeast or 2 level teaspoons fresh dried yeast (see note on page 60)
½ level teaspoon castor sugar
100 ml (3½fl oz) warm milk
225 g (8oz) plain flour, sifted
½ level teaspoon salt
25 g (1oz) butter or margarine
1 small egg, well beaten
GLAZE
1 level tablespoon castor sugar
1 tablespoon milk

1 Mix the fresh yeast and sugar together and pour on the warm milk, or dissolve the sugar in the warm milk and sprinkle over the dried yeast; leave about 20 minutes until frothy.
2 Place the flour in a bowl with the salt, rub in the butter finely.
3 When the yeast is frothy, pour it into the centre of the flour with the egg. Mix together, turn on to a floured surface and knead gently until smooth and elastic, for about 10 minutes.
4 Lightly oil a 15 cm (6in) cake tin, place in the dough and flatten slightly with the back of the hand to help fill the tin. Cover with oiled polythene and put in a warm place until the dough reaches the top of the tin (about 30-40 minutes).
5 When the dough has reached about three quarters of the way up the tin, preheat a moderately hot oven (200 deg C, 400 deg F, Gas 6), centre shelf.
6 Cook for about 20 minutes until golden brown, and sounds hollow when tapped on the base.
7 Meanwhile, dissolve the sugar for the glaze with the milk, brush over the top of the dough when cooked and return to the oven for one minute. If liked, the Sally Lunn can be turned out of the tin, glazed all over and put back in the oven for one minute.
8 Allow to cool before serving with butter. If not served at once, it can be toasted.

SHORT-TIME TEA BUN

(Makes 8 wedges)

15 g (½oz) fresh yeast
100 ml (4fl oz) tepid milk
½ (25 mg) ascorbic acid (Vitamin C) tablet
250 g (9oz) strong plain white flour
½ level teaspoon sugar
½ level teaspoon salt
15 g (½oz) margarine
75 g (3oz) currants
1 egg, beaten
GLAZE
2 level teaspoons sugar
2 tablespoons water

1 Blend the yeast in the warm milk and dissolve the ascorbic acid tablet. Leave on one side until frothy (takes about 10-20 minutes).
2 Put the flour, sugar and salt in a large bowl and rub in the margarine, add the currants.
3 Using a wooden fork mix the yeast liquid and beaten egg into the dry ingredients until the sides of the bowl are clean, a little extra flour may be needed.
4 Knead the dough until smooth and elastic, for about 10 minutes.
5 Shape the dough into a ball and place inside an oiled polythene bag for 10 minutes to relax.
6 Turn the dough on to the work surface and knead for a few minutes so that you remove all the air bubbles. Form into a ball.
7 Place on a greased baking sheet and flatten to an 18 cm (7in) round. Slash with a sharp knife into 8 sections. Cover with oiled polythene and leave in a warm place until double in size (20-30 minutes).
8 Preheat a moderately hot oven (200 deg C, 400 deg F, Gas 6), shelf above centre. Remove polythene and bake bun for 20-25 minutes until golden brown and sounds hollow when tapped on the base.
9 Meanwhile, make the glaze: dissolve the sugar in the water, bring to the boil, boil for one minute.
10 As soon as the bun is removed from the oven, place on a wire rack and brush glaze over the hot bun.
Note: *If 25 mg ascorbic acid tablets are not available, use a quarter of a 50 mg tablet.*

ALMOND AND CARDAMOM CROWN

(Serves 10)
350 g (12oz) plain flour
¼ level teaspoon salt
about 175 ml (7fl oz) milk
50 g (2oz) castor sugar
2 level teaspoons dried yeast
200 g (7oz) butter
FILLING
40 g (1½oz) butter
40 g (1½oz) icing sugar
25 g (1oz) chopped almonds
1 level teaspoon ground cardamom
TOPPING
2-3 tablespoons glacé icing
about 15 g (½oz) flaked almonds, lightly toasted

1 Sift the flour and salt into a bowl.
2 Warm the milk, stir in 1 level teaspoon of the castor sugar and sprinkle the yeast on the surface. Stand in a warm place until the yeast is frothy, about 20 minutes.
3 Mix remaining sugar into the flour. Add the yeast mixture and mix together first with a fork and then by hand. Add more milk if the mixture is too dry or a little flour if too sticky.
4 Turn out on to a surface and knead for 5-10 minutes until smooth and elastic. Wrap in oiled polythene. Chill for 15 minutes.
5 Roll out to an oblong, about 20 cm by 38 cm (8in by 15in). Place lengthwise away from you, dot the butter all over.
6 Fold in three, by folding the top third over the centre third and the bottom third over the centre. Give the pastry a quarter turn and roll and fold it again. Chill for 15 minutes, repeat rolling and folding twice more.
7 Wrap and chill overnight.
8 Next day, prepare the filling: Cream the butter and icing sugar together. Stir in the chopped almonds and cardamom.
9 Roll out the pastry to an oblong, 18 cm by 36 cm (7in by 14in).
10 Spread the filling on the pastry to within 1 cm (½in) of the edges and roll up to make a long sausage. Lift the roll on to a greased baking sheet, shaping the dough into a circle and joining the ends together. With a sharp knife, make cuts two-thirds through the pastry around the outside edge at 5 cm (2in) intervals.
11 Cover with greased polythene and put in a warm place until the dough has risen and is doubled in size.
12 Preheat a hot oven (220 deg C, 425 deg F, Gas 7), shelf above centre.
13 Remove the polythene. Bake the crown for about 20 minutes until golden and cooked through. Remove from the oven and transfer to a wire rack.
14 When cold, spoon over the glacé icing and sprinkle with almonds. Allow the icing to set before serving.

HAZELNUT DANISH PASTRIES

(Makes 16)

DOUGH
15 g (½oz) fresh yeast, or 2 level teaspoons fresh dried
    yeast (see note on page 60) and ½ teaspoon castor sugar
5 tablespoons warm water
225 g (8oz) plain flour, sifted
pinch of salt
15 g (½oz) castor sugar
25 g (1oz) lard
1 egg, beaten
150 g (5oz) butter
1 egg yolk beaten with 1 teaspoon water for glazing
HAZELNUT FILLING
100 g (4oz) hazelnuts, finely ground
100 g (4oz) castor sugar
2 level teaspoons flour
1 egg white, lightly beaten
2 teaspoons lemon juice
glacé icing (optional)
toasted chopped hazelnuts for decoration

1 **To make the dough:** Blend the fresh yeast with the warm water, or dissolve ½ teaspoon sugar in the warm water and sprinkle over the dried yeast. Leave until frothy (10-20 minutes).
2 Meanwhile, place the flour, salt and sugar in a bowl and rub in the lard. Pour in the yeast liquid and egg and mix to a soft dough.
3 Turn on to a lightly floured surface, knead gently until smooth. Place the dough in a lightly oiled polythene bag, leave to rest in a cool place for 10 minutes only.
4 Roll out the dough to an approximate 25 cm (10in) square. Press the butter in the hands to about 1 cm (½in) thick. Place down the centre of the pastry, fold the sides over to overlap by about 1 cm (½in).
5 Roll into a strip 45 cm by 41 cm (18in by 16in), fold evenly into three. Return the dough to the oiled bag to rest 10 minutes in a cool place.
6 Roll and fold the dough twice more resting it for 10 minutes between each rolling.
7 **To make the hazelnut filling:** Mix the hazelnuts, sugar, flour, egg white and the lemon juice together.
8 Cut the dough in half and roll out each piece to about 20 cm by 41 cm (8in by 16in) and then cut into 10 cm (4in) squares.
9 Divide the hazelnut mixture into 16 portions, place one in the centre of each square.
10 Lightly brush each square with egg yolk, fold over to make an oblong. Make 8 cuts along the long, sealed edges of each.
11 Place on two well greased baking sheets, brush with egg yolk and cover with oiled polythene. Put to prove in a warm atmosphere for about 20 minutes until puffy.
12 Meanwhile, preheat a hot oven (220 deg C, 425 deg F, Gas 7), shelves above and below centre.
13 Bake for 12-15 minutes until golden brown. Allow to cool, then pour a little glacé icing over (if liked) and sprinkle with a few toasted chopped hazelnuts.

65

DANISH BUTTER CAKE

(Cuts into 8 slices)

150 ml (5fl oz) milk and water mixed
1 level teaspoon sugar
25 g (1oz) fresh yeast
450 g (1lb) plain flour
1 level teaspoon salt
1 level teaspoon ground cardamom or mixed spice
50 g (2oz) castor sugar
275 g (10oz) soft butter
2 eggs, beaten
FILLING
50 g (2oz) butter
50 g (2oz) castor sugar
1 teaspoon vanilla essence
1 level teaspoon ground cinnamon
½ level teaspoon mixed spice
beaten egg white to glaze
ICING
225 g (8oz) icing sugar, sifted
2 tablespoons lemon juice, strained
shredded almonds (optional)

1 Pour the lukewarm milk and water into a small bowl, stir in the sugar and crumble in the yeast. Mix well and leave in a warm place until frothy (15-20 minutes).
2 Sift the flour, salt, cardamom, or mixed spice, and sugar into a mixing bowl. Rub in 50 g (2oz) of the butter. Make a hollow in the centre.
3 Pour the yeast liquid and the eggs into the hollow and, using fingers, mix to a fairly soft dough. Turn the dough on to a floured surface and knead well for about 10 minutes until smooth and elastic. Place the dough in a clean bowl, sprinkle with a little flour, cover and put in the refrigerator for about ½ hour.
4 Place remaining 225 g (8oz) butter between 2 sheets of kitchen foil and roll out to an oblong 13 cm by 20 cm (5in by 8in). Chill.
5 Roll the chilled dough into an oblong 30 cm by 23 cm (12in by 9in). Remove the foil from the butter and place in the centre of the dough. Fold the dough over to completely enclose the butter.
6 Roll the dough out into a strip 15 cm by 46 cm (6in by 18in). Fold the bottom third of the dough over the centre third and fold the top third down. Press the edges together to seal. Chill 20 minutes.
7 Repeat step 6 twice more. Then wrap the dough and chill for one hour.
8 To make the filling: Cream the butter with the sugar, vanilla essence, cinnamon and spice until light and fluffy.
9 Preheat a moderately hot oven (200 deg C, 400 deg F, Gas 6), centre shelf. Butter a 23 cm (9in) round, loose-based cake tin.
10 Cut off one-third of the dough, roll out into a round large enough to fit the tin. Lift into the tin and press out evenly to fit.
11 Roll remaining dough into a 46 cm (18in) square. Spread the filling over one half and fold the other over, press the edges together to seal.

12 Cut the dough into 9 equal strips, 5 cm by 23 cm (2in by 9in) and brush with beaten egg white. Roll up each strip.
13 Place 8 rolls around the edge of the tin with the remaining one in the centre. Brush with egg white. Bake for 40-45 minutes until the top is golden and crisp. Remove from the tin and place on a wire rack.
14 To make the icing: Mix the sugar with the lemon juice to make a thick coating consistency. Trickle the icing over the warm cake. If liked, scatter with shredded almonds. Serve cold.

See picture opposite

HUNGARIAN CAKEBREAD

(Cuts into 6 slices)

15 g (½oz) fresh yeast
100 ml (4fl oz) tepid milk
½ (25 mg) ascorbic acid (Vitamin C) tablet
275 g (9oz) plain white flour
½ level teaspoon salt
1 level teaspoon sugar
25 g (1oz) butter or margarine
1 level teaspoon cinnamon
1 egg, beaten
COATING
50 g (2oz) butter
75 g (3oz) soft brown sugar
1 level teaspoon cinnamon
25 g (1oz) chopped walnuts
25 g (1oz) raisins

1 Blend the yeast into the warm milk and dissolve the ascorbic acid tablet. Leave until frothy (20 minutes).
2 Put the flour, salt and sugar into a large bowl, rub in the butter, stir in the cinnamon.
3 Using a wooden fork, stir the yeast liquid and egg into the flour mixture, until the sides of the bowl are clean.
4 Knead the dough until smooth and elastic, about 10 minutes.
5 Shape the dough into a ball and place in a lightly oiled polythene bag for 10 minutes to relax.
6 To make the coating: Melt the butter in a small pan. Mix the remaining coating ingredients together, place on a piece of greaseproof paper.
7 Divide the dough into roughly 24 equal pieces. Roll each into a ball and coat with melted butter. Toss each ball in the coating ingredients.
8 Arrange a double row round a 20-23 cm (8-9in) greased ring mould. Mix any remaining butter and coating ingredients together and arrange over the top.
9 Place inside an oiled polythene bag and allow to rise until double in size (30-40 minutes).
10 Preheat a moderately hot oven (200 deg C, 400 deg F, Gas 6), centre shelf. Remove polythene. Bake for 25-30 minutes until golden brown. Remove from the tin immediately, loosening the sides if necessary. To serve, break apart with two forks.

Note: *If 25 mg ascorbic acid tablets are not available, use a quarter of a 50 mg tablet.*

66

Danish Butter Cake, *see opposite*

chapter 8
Teabreads

**The delicious little loaves that are made without yeast –
they may be sweet or savoury, with flavourings of fruit
and cheese, of nuts and spices**

WALNUT AND DATE TEABREAD

(Cuts into 10 slices)

50 g (2oz) golden syrup
25 g (1oz) black treacle
50 g (2oz) butter or margarine
150 ml (5fl oz) milk
75 g (3oz) chopped dates, rolled in sugar
225 g (8oz) self-raising flour, sifted
½ level teaspoon baking powder, sifted
½ level teaspoon cinnamon, sifted
75 g (3oz) chopped walnuts
1 large egg, well beaten
1 level tablespoon demerara sugar (optional)

1 Preheat a warm oven (170 deg C, 325 deg F, Gas 3),
centre shelf. Grease a 1½-litre (2½-pint) loaf tin and line
with greased greaseproof paper.
2 Place the syrup, treacle, butter, milk and dates in a
medium-sized saucepan. Heat gently until the butter has
just melted.
3 Remove pan from the heat and quickly fold in the flour,
baking powder, cinnamon, chopped walnuts and egg.
4 Pour into the prepared tin, level the surface, sprinkle
with demerara sugar if liked.
5 Cook for one hour until a fine skewer pushed into the
centre comes out clean.
6 Leave in the tin for 5 minutes. Turn out on to a wire
rack, remove the paper, allow to cool.
7 Serve the teabread sliced, and if liked, spread with
butter.

See picture on page 15

CARROT AND PEANUT TEA LOAF

(Cuts into about 12 slices)

225 g (8oz) self-raising flour
¼ level teaspoon salt
½ level teaspoon ground cinnamon
¼ level teaspoon baking powder
2 level teaspoons castor sugar
25 g (1oz) soft margarine
225 g (8oz) carrot, coarsely grated
75 g (3oz) salted peanuts, well chopped
1 large egg, beaten
150 ml (5fl oz) milk

1 Preheat a moderately hot oven (190 deg C, 375 deg F,
Gas 5), shelf above centre. Grease a 1½-litre (2½-pint) loaf
tin.
2 Sift the flour with the salt, cinnamon, baking powder
and sugar. Rub in the margarine.
3 Stir in the grated carrot and all but one tablespoon of
the chopped peanuts, then mix with the egg and sufficient milk to give a dropping consistency.
4 Spoon the mixture into the tin. Sprinkle the remaining
peanuts over the top. Bake for 50 minutes until golden.
5 Cool in the tin. Finish cooling on a wire rack.
6 Store overnight before serving sliced and buttered.
Good with cheeses, celery or watercress.

*It is important to follow **either** the metric **or** the imperial weights
and measures in any one recipe*

SPICED APPLE TEABREAD

(Cuts into 10-12 slices)
350 g (12oz) self-raising flour
½ level teaspoon salt
¼ level teaspoon ground allspice
½ level teaspoon grated nutmeg
75 g (3oz) castor sugar
2 large eggs
50 g (2oz) butter or margarine, melted
6 tablespoons milk
275 g (10oz) cooking or dessert apples, grated
50 g (2oz) dates, chopped
TOPPING (optional)
a few thin slices of dessert apple
honey to glaze

1 Preheat a warm oven (170 deg C, 325 deg F, Gas 3), centre shelf. Grease a 1½-litre (2½-pint) loaf tin.
2 Sift together the flour, salt and spices into a bowl. Mix in the sugar.
3 Beat the eggs in a bowl and blend in the melted butter and milk.
4 Stir the liquid ingredients into the flour mixture. Add the grated apple and chopped dates and stir well. The mixture should be of a soft dropping consistency.
5 Turn into the prepared loaf tin, smooth over the top. Bake for about 1¼ hours, or until lightly brown, and when a metal skewer inserted in the centre comes out clean. Turn out and cool on a wire rack.
6 If liked, brush the top of the loaf with warmed honey, arrange apple slices on top and brush with a little more warmed honey.

SOMERSET TEABREAD

(Cuts into 12 slices)
350 g (12oz) mixed dried fruit
50 g (2oz) glace cherries, quartered
175 ml (6fl oz) cider
125 g (4oz) soft brown sugar
1 large egg, beaten
175 g (6oz) plain flour
2 level teaspoons baking powder

1 Soak the mixed fruit and the glacé cherries in the cider overnight.
2 Preheat a warm oven (170 deg C, 325 deg F, Gas 3), centre shelf. Well-grease a 1-litre (1½-pint) loaf tin.
3 Add the sugar, beaten egg, sifted flour and baking powder to the soaked fruit.
4 Turn the mixture into the loaf tin, level the surface and bake for 1½ hours, until firm to touch. Cool on a wire rack.
5 Serve sliced and buttered.

COTTAGE TEABREAD

(Cuts into 8 slices)
225 g (8oz) self-raising flour
¼ level teaspsoon salt
50 g (2oz) butter or margarine
125 g (4oz) cottage cheese
50 g (2oz) walnuts, finely chopped
25 g (1oz) castor sugar
1 egg, beaten
5 tablespoons milk

1 Preheat a moderate oven (180 deg C, 350 deg F, Gas 4), centre shelf. Grease or oil a 1-litre (1½-pint) loaf tin.
2 Place the flour and salt in a mixing bowl and rub in the butter until crumbly and fine.
3 Add the cottage cheese, walnuts and sugar. Mix well.
4 Mix the egg with the milk and pour into the dry ingredients. Mix to a soft batter.
5 Transfer to the tin and level the surface.
6 Bake for 50-60 minutes until risen and lightly browned and a skewer inserted in the centre comes out clean.
7 Turn out carefully and leave to cool on a wire rack.
8 Serve sliced and buttered with honey or cheese.

RAISIN AND BANANA BREAD

(Cuts into about 12 slices)
175 g (6oz) self-raising flour
½ level teaspoon baking powder
¼ level teaspoon salt
50 g (2oz) wholemeal flour
125 g (4oz) butter
75 g (3oz) demerara sugar
175 g (6oz) raisins
450 g (1lb) bananas, peeled and mashed
2 eggs, beaten
finely grated rind ½ lemon

1 Preheat a moderate oven (180 deg C, 350 deg F, Gas 4), centre shelf. Grease a 1¼-litre (2-pint) loaf tin and line with greased greaseproof paper.
2 Sift the self-raising flour, baking powder and salt into a bowl. Stir in the wholemeal flour and rub in the butter until the mixture resembles breadcrumbs.
3 Mix in the sugar, raisins, bananas, eggs and lemon rind and beat lightly until well mixed. Spoon into the tin.
4 Bake for 1-1¼ hours until just firm to touch. Turn out of the tin and remove the paper, cool on a wire rack. Serve sliced and buttered.

Note: *This bread keeps well wrapped in foil in an airtight container for up to one week.*

Top: **Advocaat Dessert Cake,** *see page 41. Above:* **Mint and Lemon Tea Cake,** *see page 72*

70

Ginger Sodabread, *see page 72*

GINGER SODABREAD

(Cuts into 12 pieces)
225 g (8oz) plain wholemeal flour
1 level teaspoon baking powder
½ level teaspoon bicarbonate of soda
1½-2 level teaspoons ground ginger
1 level tablespoon cocoa malt drink powder (such as Bournvita)
¼ level teaspoon salt
125 g (4oz) butter or margarine
2 level tablespoons black treacle
75 g (3oz) soft brown sugar
1 egg, beaten
175 ml (6fl oz) milk and water
TOPPING
1 level tablespoon treacle
40 g (1½oz) crystallised ginger

1 Preheat a moderate oven (180 deg C, 350 deg F, Gas 4), centre shelf. Brush an 18 cm by 28 cm (7in by 11in) tin with oil and line the base with greased greaseproof paper.
2 Mix together the flour, baking powder, bicarbonate of soda, ginger, malt drink powder and salt in a mixing bowl.
3 Put the butter, black treacle and sugar in a saucepan and warm gently until the butter has melted.
4 Mix the egg with the milk and water.
5 Add all these ingredients to the dry mixture, and stir well until blended.
6 Pour into the prepared tin, and level the top. Bake for about 25 minutes, until firm and mixture begins to leave sides of the tin. Turn out and cool on a wire rack.
7 **To make the topping:** Warm the treacle and brush it over the cake.
8 Chop the crystallised ginger finely, and sprinkle over the top, pressing into place. Cut the cake into squares.
See picture on page 71

MINT AND LEMON TEA CAKE

(Cuts into 8 slices)
350 g (12oz) self-raising flour
1 level teaspoon salt
175 g (6oz) butter
175 g (6oz) castor sugar
grated rind 1 medium-sized lemon
1 level teaspoon dried mint
2 eggs
5 tablespoons milk
ICING
100 g (4oz) icing sugar
8 teaspoons lemon juice, strained
DECORATION
mixed glacé fruits

1 Preheat a moderate oven (180 deg C, 350 deg F, Gas 4), shelf just above centre. Well-grease a 1½-litre (2½-pint) loaf tin and line with greased greaseproof paper.
2 Sift the flour and salt into a bowl. Rub in the butter. Add the sugar, lemon rind and mint. Toss well. Using a fork, mix to a stiffish batter with the eggs and milk.
3 Spread smoothly into the prepared tin. Bake for one hour until firm to the touch. Leave in the tin 10 minutes. Turn out on to a wire cooling rack. Peel away the lining paper and leave the cake until completely cold.
4 **To make the icing:** Sift the sugar into a bowl and mix to a smooth coating consistency with the lemon juice. Spread over the top of the cake allowing it to trickle partially down the sides. When firm, decorate to taste.
See picture on page 70

HIGHLAND GINGERBREAD

(Cuts into 10 pieces)
125 g (4oz) margarine
75 g (3oz) soft brown sugar
175 g (6oz) black treacle
125 g (4oz) golden syrup
1 level teaspoon ground ginger
½ level teaspoon ground cloves
½ level teaspoon cinnamon
100 ml (4fl oz) milk
2 eggs
½ level teaspoon bicarbonate of soda
1 tablespoon hot water
225 g (8oz) plain flour
3 level tablespoons ginger marmalade

1 Preheat a warm oven (170 deg C, 325 deg F, Gas 3), centre shelf. Grease a 22 cm (8½in) square cake tin and line the base with greased greaseproof paper.
2 Warm together in a saucepan the margarine, sugar, treacle, syrup and spices. Add the milk and stir to blend.
3 Beat the eggs in a large bowl; dissolve the bicarbonate of soda in the water, and add to the eggs, together with the warmed mixture from the saucepan.

4 Stir in the flour and marmalade, beat well to mix.
5 Transfer to the tin and bake for 1½ hours, until firm to the touch.
6 Leave to cool in the tin, then turn out carefully and peel off the lining paper.
7 Store in airtight container for 2-3 days before serving.
8 Serve cut in wedges.

TREACLE GINGERBREAD

(Cuts into 12-16 pieces)
about 125 g (4oz) ginger marmalade (optional)
125 g (4oz) butter or margarine
75 g (3oz) soft brown sugar
125 g (4oz) black treacle
175 g (6oz) plain flour
1 heaped teaspoon ground ginger
1 level teaspoon ground cinnamon
150 ml (5fl oz) milk
1 level teaspoon bicarbonate of soda
1 egg, lightly beaten

1 Preheat a cool oven (150 deg C, 300 deg F, Gas 2), centre shelf. Grease an 18 cm (7in) square cake tin and line the base with greased greaseproof paper.
2 Spread the ginger marmalade (if using) over the base of the cake tin.
3 Place the butter, sugar and treacle in a saucepan and heat gently until the fat has melted. Remove the pan from the heat.
4 Sift flour with ginger and cinnamon into a large bowl.
5 Warm the milk in a small saucepan, add the bicarbonate of soda and stir to dissolve.
6 Make a well in the centre of the flour mixture and pour in the melted treacle, the milk and egg. Beat until smooth. Pour into the tin and bake for one hour until just firm when lightly pressed with the tips of the fingers, and drawing away from the sides of the tin.
7 Leave to cool in the tin, then turn out carefully and peel off the lining paper.
8 Store in airtight container 2-3 days before serving.
9 Serve cut in wedges.

SODABREAD ROLLS

(Makes 8)
15 g (½oz) butter
225 g (8oz) plain flour
½ level teaspoon salt
1 level teaspoon bicarbonate of soda
100 ml (4fl oz) buttermilk

1 Preheat a hot oven (220 deg C, 425 deg F, Gas 7), centre shelf. Lightly grease a baking sheet.
2 Rub the butter into the flour, add salt and bicarbonate of soda. Stir in buttermilk, knead to give a soft dough.
3 Divide into 8 pieces and shape into rounds or fingers.
4 Transfer to the baking sheet and cook for 10-12 minutes, until the rolls are cooked and sound hollow when tapped on the bases.

FRUIT AND NUT GINGERBREAD

(Cuts into 12 pieces)
275 g (10oz) self-raising flour
200 g (7oz) demerara sugar
2 level teaspoons ground ginger
1 level teaspoon cinnamon
¼ level teaspoon salt
2 rounded tablespoons black treacle
150 ml (5fl oz) corn oil
2 large eggs
50 g (2oz) blanched almonds
50 g (2oz) seedless raisins
50 g (2oz) chopped mixed peel

1 Preheat a moderate oven (180 deg C, 350 deg F, Gas 4), shelf above centre. Grease a 1½-litre (2½-pint) loaf tin.
2 Place the flour, sugar, ginger, cinnamon and salt in a mixing bowl and stir to mix.
3 Warm the treacle in a small pan over gentle heat. Add the oil and mix together.
4 Make a well in the centre of the dry ingredients, pour in the liquid and mix well. Beat in the eggs one at a time. Beat in the almonds, raisins and peel.
5 Turn the mixture into the prepared tin, bake for about one hour until the top is firm to touch. Cool the gingerbread on a wire rack.
6 Store in airtight container 2-3 days before serving.

WHOLEMEAL SODABREAD

(Makes 4 quarters)
25 g (1oz) butter
350 g (12oz) plain wholemeal flour
1 level teaspoon salt
1 level teaspoon baking powder
½ level teaspoon bicarbonate of soda
275 ml (½ pint) buttermilk

1 Preheat a hot oven (220 deg C, 425 deg F, Gas 7), centre shelf. Lightly oil an 18 cm (7in) sandwich tin.
2 Rub the butter into the flour, add the salt and sift in the baking powder and bicarbonate of soda.
3 Stir in the buttermilk with a wooden fork or spoon.
4 Turn on to a lightly floured surface, knead gently to make into a round, place in the tin. Level the surface with the knuckles. Score the top in four.
5 Cook for ½ hour until risen and brown. Turn on to a wire rack to cool.

WALNUT, RAISIN
AND CHEESE LOAF

(Cuts into 10 slices)

350 g (12oz) self-raising flour
½ level teaspoon salt
pinch of cayenne pepper
½ level teaspoon dry mustard
75 g (3oz) butter or margarine
75 g (3oz) mature Cheddar cheese, finely grated
75 g (3oz) raisins
50 g (2oz) chopped walnuts
1 egg, beaten
250 ml (½ pint) milk
TOPPING
15 g (½oz) mature Cheddar cheese, finely grated
15 g (½oz) chopped walnuts

1 Preheat a moderate oven (180 deg C, 350 deg F, Gas 4), centre shelf. Grease a 1½-litre (2½-pint) loaf tin.
2 Sift the flour, salt, cayenne pepper and mustard into a bowl. Add the butter, rub in finely.
3 Stir in the cheese, raisins and walnuts. Mix in the egg and milk and beat well.
4 Turn the mixture into the prepared tin and level the surface. Mix the topping ingredients together with a fork, sprinkle over the loaf.
5 Bake for 1¼-1½ hours or until a skewer inserted in the centre comes out clean.
6 Turn out and cool on a wire rack. Serve sliced and buttered.
See picture opposite

RISE AND SHINE LOAF

(Cuts into 10-12 slices)

225 g (8oz) self-raising flour
1 level teaspoon baking powder
100 g (4oz) All Bran breakfast cereal
2 well-rounded tablespoons thick honey
2 well-rounded tablespoons golden syrup
2 well-rounded tablespoons marmalade
150 ml (5fl oz) natural yogurt
100 g (4oz) raisins
75 ml (3fl oz) milk

1 Preheat a moderate oven (180 deg C, 350 deg F, Gas 4), centre shelf. Grease a 1½-litre (2½-pint) loaf tin.
2 Sift the flour and baking powder into a large bowl, stir in the bran then make a hollow in the centre.
3 Add the honey, syrup, marmalade, yogurt, raisins and half the milk. Mix together adding sufficient extra milk to give the mixture a soft dropping consistency.
4 Turn the mixture into the loaf tin. Bake for about 1¼ hours until the loaf is risen and cooked through.
5 Turn on to a wire rack to cool.

Walnut, Raisin and Cheese Loaf, *see opposite*

chapter 9
Scones

Always traditional teatime favourites, served with butter and jam and sometimes cream – now they may be lunch or supper snacks with cheese, bacon, even curry flavours

PARMESAN AND BACON SCONES

(Makes about 10)
225 g (8oz) self-raising flour
½ level teaspoon bicarbonate of soda
1 level teaspoon cream of tartar
50 g (2oz) butter or margarine
25 g (1oz) Parmesan cheese
50 g (2oz) streaky bacon
150 ml (5fl oz) milk
milk to glaze

1 Preheat a hot oven (220 deg C, 425 deg F, Gas 7), shelf above centre. Grease a baking sheet.
2 Sift together the flour, bicarbonate of soda and cream of tartar. Add the butter and rub in, using the fingertips, until the mixture resembles fine crumbs.
3 Add most of the Parmesan cheese keeping back a little for sprinkling on top of the scones.
4 Remove the rind from the rashers, chop the bacon finely and fry quickly until cooked. Drain the bacon on kitchen paper, add to the scone mixture.
5 Add the milk and stir with a knife to form a soft but not sticky dough.
6 Turn on to a lightly floured surface and knead gently to form a smooth ball.
7 Roll out to about 1.5 cm (½in) thick, then cut into rounds with a 6 cm (2¼in) cutter. Place these on the baking sheet.
8 Brush with milk and sprinkle with the remaining cheese.
9 Bake for 12-15 minutes until the scones are well risen and golden brown.
10 Serve while still warm.

TASTY-TOPPED CHEESE SCONES

(Cuts into 32 half-scones)
350 g (12oz) self-raising flour
¼ level teaspoon salt
75 g (3oz) margarine
75 g (3oz) Cheddar cheese, grated
225 ml (8fl oz) milk
SALMON AND OLIVE TOPPING
50 g (2oz) butter, softened
78 g (2.75oz) jar salmon and shrimp paste
75 g (3oz) stuffed olives
TANGY HERB TOPPING
100 g (4oz) butter, softened
1 rounded teaspoon yeast extract
1 rounded teaspoon chopped chives
2 rounded teapoons chopped parsley
2 medium-sized tomatoes
parsley for garnish

1 Preheat a hot oven (220 deg C, 425 deg F, Gas 7), towards top and centre shelves. Grease two baking sheets.
2 Sift the flour and salt into a bowl. Rub in the margarine until the mixture resembles breadcrumbs. Stir in the cheese and add enough of the milk to make a soft but not sticky dough.
3 Roll out the dough on a lightly floured surface to 2 cm (¾in) thick. With a biscuit cutter, cut sixteen 6 cm (2¼in) rounds and place on the baking sheets. Brush the tops with milk. Cook for 10-12 minutes until well risen and golden brown. Lift on to a wire rack to cool.
4 **To make the salmon and olive topping:** Cream the butter well and beat in the paste. Reserve 8 olives for

decoration; chop the remainder and mix into the butter and paste mixture.

5 To make the tangy herb topping: Cream the butter well, then add the yeast extract and chopped chives and chopped parsley.

6 Split the scones.

7 Spread half the scone halves with salmon and olive topping. Cut the reserved olives in two and place a half on top of each topped scone half.

8 Spread the remaining scone halves with the tangy herb topping. Thinly slice each tomato into eight and place a slice on each scone half, plus a small sprig of parsley.

CURRIED CHEESE SCONES

(Makes about 26)
450 g (1lb) self-raising flour
2 level teaspoons baking powder
1 level teaspoon salt
100 g (4oz) margarine
175 g (6oz) sharp Cheddar cheese, finely grated
2 level teaspoons dry mustard
2 level teaspoons curry powder
250 ml (½ pint) milk

1 Preheat a hot oven (220 deg C, 425 deg F, Gas 7), shelves above and below centre. Grease two baking sheets.

2 Sift the flour, baking powder and salt, rub in the margarine until crumbly. Stir in 100 g (4oz) cheese. Add the mustard and curry powder and mix.

3 Use sufficient milk to bind to a soft but not sticky dough.

4 Roll out on a floured surface to 1.5 cm (½in) thick then cut into 5-6 cm (2in) rounds. Place on the baking sheets. Sprinkle with the remaining cheese.

5 Bake for 10-15 minutes or until they are well risen and cooked through.

6 Serve hot or cold with butter.

SAVOURY SCONES WITH PEANUT SPREAD

(Makes 12)
225 g (8oz) plain flour
1 level teaspoon bicarbonate of soda
1 level teaspoon cream of tartar
50 g (2oz) butter or margarine
150 ml (5fl oz) buttermilk
1 level teaspoon meat extract
PEANUT SPREAD
1 small packet of salted peanuts, finely chopped
75 g (3oz) cream cheese
1 teaspoon oil
2 teaspoons milk

1 Preheat a hot oven (220 deg C, 425 deg F, Gas 7), shelf above centre. Grease a baking sheet.

2 Sift the flour with the bicarbonate of soda and cream of tartar. Rub in the butter until the mixture resembles fine breadcrumbs.

3 Place the buttermilk in a small bowl. Add the meat extract and whisk to dissolve.

4 Make a well in the dry ingredients, pour in most of the liquid and mix to a soft dough with a spatula or knife. Use all the buttermilk if necessary.

5 Turn the dough out on to a floured surface, knead very lightly with the fingertips.

6 Divide the dough into 2 balls and roll each into a round about 15 cm (6in) in diameter.

7 Place on baking sheet and cut each round into 6 wedges.

8 Bake for about 15 minutes or until golden brown.

9 To make the peanut spread: Place all the ingredients in a small bowl and mix well.

10 Serve scones warm with butter and peanut spread.

SWEET SCONES

(Makes about 10)
225 g (8oz) self-raising flour
25 g (1oz) castor sugar
25 g (1oz) margarine
25 g (1oz) cooking fat
150 ml (5fl oz) milk or milk and water
a little milk for glazing

1 Preheat a hot oven (220 deg C, 425 deg F, Gas 7), shelf above centre. Grease a baking sheet.

2 Sift the flour into a bowl, stir in the sugar. Rub in the margarine and cooking fat until the mixture is crumbly.

3 Add the liquid and mix to a soft dough.

4 Roll out on a floured board, to 1.5 cm (½in) thickness, and then cut the dough into rounds with a 5 cm (2in) fluted biscuit cutter.

5 Place the rounds on the baking sheet, brush the tops with milk and cook for 15-20 minutes, until well risen and brown.

6 Cool on a wire rack.

7 Serve with butter and jam.

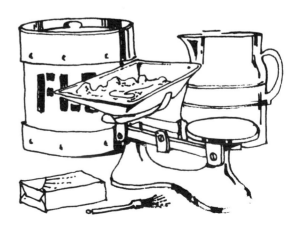

TREACLE WHOLEWHEAT SCONES

(Makes about 12)
125 g (4oz) wholewheat flour
125 g (4oz) plain flour
¼ level teaspoon salt
4 level teaspoons baking powder
½ level teaspoon mixed spice
25 g (1oz) castor sugar
25 g (1oz) lard or margarine
1 rounded tablespoon black treacle
about 125 ml (4fl oz) milk

1 Preheat a hot oven (220 deg C, 425 deg F, Gas 7), shelf above centre. Lightly grease a baking sheet.
2 Put the wholewheat flour in a mixing bowl. Sift in the plain flour, salt, baking powder, mixed spice and sugar.
3 Cut in the fat and rub in finely. Make a hollow in the centre.
4 Add the treacle and milk and mix to a soft but not sticky dough. Turn out on to a floured surface and knead lightly.
5 Roll the dough out to about 1.5 cm (½in) thick. Stamp out into 6 cm (2¼in) rounds, using a biscuit cutter.
6 Place on the baking sheet and bake for about 15 minutes until well risen and golden brown. Cool on a wire rack.
7 Serve warm or cold with butter.

HONEY AND WALNUT SCONES

(Makes 12)
225 g (8oz) self-raising flour, sifted
25 g (1oz) margarine
25 g (1oz) lard
25 g (1oz) walnuts, chopped
2 level tablespoons honey
5 tablespoons milk
milk to glaze

1 Preheat a hot oven (220 deg C, 425 deg F, Gas 7), shelf above centre. Lightly sprinkle a baking sheet with flour.
2 Rub the margarine and lard into the flour. Add the chopped walnuts.
3 Stir together the honey and milk and, using a knife, mix this liquid into the dry ingredients to make a soft dough.
4 Turn on to a floured surface and knead lightly until smooth.
5 Roll out to about 1.5 cm (½in) thick and cut into rounds with a 6 cm (2¼in) cutter.
6 Place on the baking sheet and brush the tops with milk to glaze.
7 Bake for about 15 minutes, until the scones are risen and golden.
8 Serve the scones hot or cold, split in half and spread generously with butter.

CINNAMON RING-AROUND

(Makes 2 rings)
450 g (1lb) self-raising flour
2 level teaspoons baking powder
1 level teaspoon salt
100 g (4oz) margarine
75 g (3oz) castor sugar
1 egg
250 ml (½ pint) milk
2-3 level teaspoons cinnamon
1-2 tablespoons castor sugar

1 Preheat a hot oven (220 deg C, 425 deg F, Gas 7), shelf above centre. Grease two baking sheets.
2 Sift the flour, baking powder and salt together, rub in margarine until crumbly. Stir in 75 g (3oz) castor sugar.
3 Whisk the egg and add to the milk. Use all but about 2 tablespoons to bind to a soft but not sticky dough.
4 Halve the mixture, roll each piece into a roughly oblong shape. Brush the surface of the dough with beaten egg and milk and sprinkle with most of the cinnamon and castor sugar.
5 Roll up like Swiss rolls. Curl the rolls round to form 2 rings. Press the ends together.
6 Brush the tops with the rest of the egg and milk. Sprinkle with the rest of the cinnamon and sugar. Make shallow slits diagonally through the dough.
7 Bake about 20 minutes until cooked through. Cool on a wire rack.
8 Serve sliced with butter.

SCOTCH PANCAKES

(Makes 18)
lard for greasing
225 g (8oz) plain flour
3 level teaspoons baking powder
25 g (1oz) castor sugar
2 eggs
225 ml (8fl oz) milk

1 Put a lightly greased griddle, or very large heavy based frying pan, on a medium heat, or use an electric frying pan.
2 Sift the flour, baking powder and sugar into a mixing bowl. Make a well in the centre and add the eggs. Gradually beat the eggs into the flour, adding the milk as the mixture thickens. Continue to beat in the milk until it is all used up. Then beat the mixture well.
3 Drop tablespoons of the pancake mixture on to the hot griddle, or into the frying pan, spacing well apart. Cook gently for 1-2 minutes, until bubbles appear on the surface. Turn the pancakes over and cook the other side for 1-2 minutes.
4 Keep the first batch warm while you are cooking the remaining mixture.
5 Serve at once with butter, and with jam if liked.

78

GRIDDLE SCONES

(Makes 18)

lard for greasing
450 g (1lb) plain flour
1 level teaspoon bicarbonate of soda
1 level teaspoon cream of tartar
3 level teaspoons baking powder
½ level teaspoon salt
75 g (3oz) castor sugar
50 g (2oz) butter or margarine
two 142 ml (5fl oz) cartons soured cream
150 ml (5fl oz) milk

1 Put a lightly greased griddle, or large heavy based frying pan, on medium heat, or use electric frying pan.

2 Sift the flour, bicarbonate of soda, cream of tartar, baking powder, salt and sugar into a mixing bowl. Rub in the butter or margarine. Mix to a soft dough with the soured cream and milk.

3 Lightly knead the dough on a floured surface and roll out to 1.5 cm (½in) thick. Cut out rounds using a 7 cm (2¾in) plain round cutter.

4 Place the scones on the heated griddle and cook over a low heat for 6-8 minutes, turn over and cook the other side for 6-8 minutes or until the scones are well risen and firm to the touch. Cool on a wire rack.

5 While the first batch of scones are cooking, re-roll the trimmings and cut out more scones, continuing until the dough is used up. Cook each batch in the same way.

6 Serve with butter and strawberry jam; and with whipped or clotted cream for a special treat. Serve on the day they are cooked.

See picture below

Griddle Scones, *see above*

chapter 10
Christmas Bakes

Pretty cakes, fun cakes, different cakes, and some little individual bakes, to make for the Christmas tea or to give away as special presents

GINGERBREAD HOUSE

GINGERBREAD
200 g (8oz) soft light brown sugar
200 g (8oz) golden syrup
100 g (4oz) margarine
2 tablespoons milk
400 g (1lb) plain flour
1 level teaspoon bicarbonate of soda
½ level teaspoon ground cinnamon
1 level tablespoon ground ginger
a large piece of stiff card

1 Put the sugar, syrup, margarine and milk in a saucepan over a gentle heat. Allow the mixture to dissolve, stirring from time to time. Don't boil. Cool for a few minutes.
2 Sift the flour, bicarbonate of soda, cinnamon and ginger into a large bowl. Make a hollow in the centre.
3 Pour in the melted mixture and mix, first with a wooden spoon and then with the hand, to a fairly firm dough. Knead until smooth.
4 Cover the dough and chill for about ½ hour until cold.
5 Meanwhile, cut pieces of card (see diagram) to use as a guide for cutting out house shapes. Cut 2 of each shape.
6 Preheat a warm oven (170 deg C, 325 deg F, Gas 3), shelves above and below centre. Lightly oil several baking sheets and/or Swiss-roll tins.
7 On a lightly floured surface, roll out the chilled dough to about 1 cm (⅜in) thick and cut out the 6 pieces for the house, using the card shapes as a guide.
8 Lift pieces on to sheets leaving spaces between.
9 Bake two sheets at a time for 15-20 minutes until a light golden colour.
10 Remove from the oven, cool one minute then, using a sharp knife and card shapes, trim the gingerbread to the original shape while still hot. Cool on wire racks.
11 When cold, store in airtight containers.
Note: *If the gingerbread feels soft when ready to assemble house, crisp up in a warm oven and cool before using.*

ROYAL ICING
4 egg whites
2 teaspoons lemon juice
about ¾ kg (1½lb) icing sugar, sifted

1 Beat the egg whites and lemon juice to a froth with a wooden spoon.
2 Add the icing sugar, a tablespoon at a time, beating well after each addition. Continue adding the icing sugar until the icing stands in firm peaks.
3 Keep icing covered with damp cloth to prevent crust.

TO DECORATE THE HOUSE
the 6 card shapes

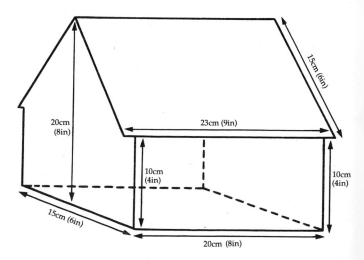

*It is important to follow **either** the metric **or** the imperial weights and measures in any one recipe*

30-36 cm (12-14 in) square board covered in foil
royal icing
the 6 cooled gingerbread house pieces
1¼ boxes Extrathin plain chocolate wafers, or chocolate buttons
1 box of 70 orange flavoured chocolate sticks
7 miniature dairy milk chocolate bars
1 tube of 20 fruit gums
4 small boiled-sweet lollies
thin strips of angelica
12 chocolate buttons ready coated in 'hundreds and thousands'
14 square-shaped liquorice allsorts (optional)

1 Using sticky tape, stick the card pieces together to form the house shape. Stand the house shape on the board.
2 Pipe or spread the sides and ends of the card house with a little of the royal icing, then put the gingerbread pieces into position and press on to the sides. Attach the roof pieces in the same way. Allow the icing to set, about one hour.
3 **To make the roof:** Pipe or spread icing along the bottom edge of one side of the roof, then arrange a line of chocolate wafers on top to represent tiles and press gently into the icing. Repeat this on the other side of the roof. Then gradually build up the tile effect in the same way until the roof is covered. Finish the top with a line of chocolate sticks.
4 **To make the chimney:** Ice a miniature chocolate bar on to either side of one end of the roof top to form a base for the chimney. Stick 5 more bars together with icing and put on to the chimney base. Top the chimney with 4 fruit gums, stuck together with more icing. Allow the icing to set, about one hour.
5 **To make the house walls:** Decorate one wall at a time. Spread the icing all over the gingerbread wall, then decoratively arrange remaining chocolate sticks for beams, window frames and doors, remaining fruit gums for windows, lollies for trees, and angelica and chocolate drops ready-coated with 'hundreds and thousands' for flowering shrubs. Press all firmly in position before starting another wall.
6 **To make the garden:** Spread the board with a thin coating of icing and make a footpath with the liquorice allsorts, if liked. Arrange any extra chocolate sticks to make a pile of wood.

Note: *For the best result, decorate the house one day before it is required. Keep it in a fairly cool room away from steam from the kitchen or excess heat from radiators and fires.*

See picture on page 83

WHITE CHRISTMAS CAKE

(Makes one large or two small cakes)
225 g (8oz) butter, softened
225 g (8oz) icing sugar, sifted
4 eggs
250 g (9oz) plain flour
½ level teaspoon baking powder
½ teaspoon vanilla essence
grated rind and juice ½ lemon

100 g (4oz) glacé cherries, quartered
100 g (4oz) glacé pineapple, chopped
100 g (4oz) shelled brazil nuts, chopped
100 g (4oz) blanched almonds, chopped
225 g (8oz) sultanas
DECORATION
apricot glaze (see recipe below)
almond paste (see recipe below)
glacé pineapple rings or chunks
glacé cherries
angelica

1 Preheat a cool oven (150 deg C, 300 deg F, Gas 2), centre shelf. Grease a 23 cm (9in) round or a 20 cm (8in) square tin, or two 15 cm (6in) round or two 13 cm (5in) square tins and line with greased greaseproof paper.
2 Cream butter and sugar until light and fluffy. Beat in eggs one at a time, beating well after each addition.
3 Sift the flour and baking powder together. Add to the mixture alternately with remaining ingredients.
4 Transfer to the prepared tins and level the surface.
5 Cook the cake for one hour, reduce the oven temperature to very cool (140 deg C, 275 deg F, Gas 1) for a further 2¼-2½ hours for the bigger cake and 1-1½ hours for the smaller cakes. Ovens vary considerably so test the cake before the end of the cooking time by inserting a fine skewer into centre. When cake is cooked, it should come out clean. If cake is overbrowning, cover with paper.
6 Allow the cake to stand for 10 minutes before turning out of the tin; cool completely before removing the paper.
7 The cake can be stored in an airtight container before decorating; it keeps well for up to a month.
8 **To decorate:** Brush the cake with hot apricot glaze. Roll out the almond paste to a size that will cover the top and sides of the cake, eg for a 23 cm (9in) round cake, roll the paste to a 30-36 cm (12-14in) round. Lift this, over a rolling pin, on to the cake. Mould the almond paste on to the cake, smooth with a palette knife and trim the base.
9 Arrange the glacé fruits on top of the cake, as liked, and fix them with warm apricot glaze.

See picture on page 82

ALMOND PASTE
(Makes 1¼ kg/2½lb)
350 g (12oz) ground almonds
350 g (12oz) castor sugar
350 g (12oz) icing sugar, sifted
2 small eggs, lightly beaten
1-2 tablespoons lemon juice, strained
1 tablespoon sherry (optional)
¼ teaspoon each vanilla and almond essence

1 Mix ground almonds, sugar and icing sugar together. Hollow out the centre and add the eggs, lemon juice, sherry (if using), and essences. Mix well and knead until free from cracks on a lightly sugared surface.
2 Put in polythene bag, store in cool place till wanted.

APRICOT GLAZE
225 g (8oz) apricot jam
juice 1 lemon

1 Heat jam and juice, stirring. Rub through a sieve.
2 Use hot. If necessary, reheat over pan of hot water.

RUM, RAISIN AND CHESTNUT CHRISTMAS CAKE

(Makes one large cake)
450 g (1lb) raisins
125 ml (4fl oz) rum
175 g (6oz) butter or margarine
125 g (4oz) soft dark brown sugar
225 g (8oz) canned sweet chestnut purée
3 eggs, separated
finely grated rind and juice ½ orange
175 g (6oz) plain flour
DECORATIONS
green food colouring
450 g (1lb) home-made or bought almond paste or
   marzipan
a little apricot jam, warmed and sieved
wide white gift-wrap ribbon, bells, silver-coloured
   'Merry Christmas' decoration

1 Place the raisins in a bowl, soak in half the rum; cover, leave overnight.
2 Preheat a warm oven (170 deg C, 325 deg F, Gas 3), shelf below centre. Grease a 1½-litre (2½-pint) loaf tin, line with greased double thickness greaseproof paper.

3 Cream the butter and sugar until light and fluffy then stir in the chestnut purée.
4 Beat in the egg yolks and orange rind and juice.
5 Fold in half the flour, then the rum-soaked raisins and remaining flour.
6 Whisk the egg whites stiffly and fold into the mixture. Turn into the prepared tin.
7 Bake for one hour then reduce oven temperature to cool (150 deg C, 300 deg F, Gas 2) and cover the top of the cake with foil. Cook for a further 1½ hours or until firm in the centre and cooked through. Cool in the tin.
8 Turn the cold cake out of the tin on to a board. Remove the paper, prick the base of the cake well with a fine skewer and spoon over the remaining rum. Wrap the cake in foil, place in airtight container for up to 4 weeks.
9 To decorate: This can be completed up to a week in advance. Knead a few drops of green colouring into the almond paste or marzipan to make a pale colour. Put aside about 50 g (2oz) then roll the rest into panels to cover the sides and top of the cake.
10 Brush the cake with the prepared jam then firmly press the marzipan pieces into position. Pinch the seams together in a neat pattern.
11 Add any marzipan trimmings to the reserved piece and knead in more green colouring to make dark green. Roll out thinly.
12 Cut a small Christmas tree the same height as the sides of the cake in kitchen foil or card. Using this guide

White Christmas Cake, *see page 81*

Gingerbread House, *see page 80*

cut out 6 Christmas trees in marzipan. Seal these on to the sides of the cake with jam.

13 Tie a decorative bow round the cake then decorate the top with bells and silver-coloured 'Merry Christmas' decoration.

SURPRISE CHRISTMAS PUDDING CAKE

(Makes 8-10 slices)

50 g (2oz) dessert chocolate
125 g (4oz) cocoa
175 g (6oz) self-raising flour
¼ level teaspoon salt
2 level teaspoons instant coffee powder
175 g (6oz) butter or margarine
175 g (6oz) castor sugar
2 eggs
75 g (3oz) icing sugar, sifted
2 teaspoons brandy, or water and brandy essence
wrapped sweets
holly for decoration

1 Preheat a warm oven (170 deg C, 325 deg F, Gas 3), centre shelf. Brush a 1¼-litre (2-pint) ovenproof pudding basin with oil and line the base with greaseproof paper.
2 Chop the chocolate into fairly small pieces.
3 Sift the cocoa, flour and salt together on to a large sheet of paper.
4 Dissolve the coffee powder in one tablespoon boiling water and then stir in 2 tablespoons cold water.
5 Cream the butter and sugar together until pale and fluffy. Gradually beat in the eggs a little at a time, beating well after each addition.
6 Lightly fold in the sifted dry ingredients and the chocolate with the dissolved coffee to give a dropping consistency.
7 Spoon the mixture into the prepared basin and cook for about 1 hour 20 minutes until risen and firm to the touch in the centre. Leave in the bowl to cool.
8 Slip a knife round the side of the cake to loosen it from the bowl. Check the cake will turn out easily; then, while it is still in the bowl scoop out a pyramid shaped portion from the centre of the cake.
9 Cut a thick slice off the base of the 'pyramid'. Put the wrapped sweets into the hole in the centre then cover them with the slice of cake.
10 Put a serving plate over the pudding basin and turn the cake out on to it.
11 Mix the icing sugar with sufficient brandy (or water and brandy essence) to give a thick icing that will only just run. Spoon over the top of the 'pudding' cake and let it trickle down slightly so it looks like brandy sauce. When the icing has set, put a sprig of holly in the centre.

HUNGARIAN CHRISTMAS CAKE

(Cuts into about 20 portions)

150 g (5oz) butter, softened
150 g (5oz) castor sugar
very finely grated rind 1 medium-sized lemon
5 large eggs, separated
150 g (5oz) ground almonds
5 tablespoons dark rum
DECORATION
icing sugar
6 glacé cherries, halved
6 walnut halves

1 Preheat a warm oven (150 deg C, 325 deg F, Gas 3), shelf below centre. Brush the base and sides of a 20 cm (8in) round cake tin with melted butter. Line completely with greaseproof paper and brush the paper with more melted butter.
2 Put the butter, sugar and lemon rind into a bowl. Cream by beating well together until very light, fluffy and almost white in colour.
3 Beat in the egg yolks, one at a time. Stir in the ground almonds alternately with the rum.
4 In a clean, dry bowl, beat the egg whites to a stiff snow. Using a metal spoon or spatula, gently and carefully cut and fold the beaten whites into the cake mixture. When smooth and evenly combined, transfer to prepared tin.
5 Bake for one hour. Cool for 15 minutes in the tin, then carefully turn out on to a tea-towel resting on a wire rack. Peel away the paper when the cake is almost cold. When cold, turn over on to a serving plate.
6 To decorate: Dust the top of the cake with sifted icing sugar, then make a centre garland of cherries and nuts.

Note: *This cake sinks on cooling, as do all cakes of this type made without flour. The texture and flavour is like that of moist marzipan.*

LAST-MINUTE CHRISTMAS CAKE

(Cuts into 16-20 slices)

125 g (4oz) butter or margarine
350 g (12oz) self-raising flour, sifted
100 g (4oz) soft dark brown sugar
finely grated rind 1 large orange
finely grated rind 1 large lemon
3 eggs
2 tablespoons brandy or milk
411 g (14½oz) jar good quality mincemeat
350 g (12oz) bought almond paste
1 tablespoon apricot jam
225 g (8oz) icing sugar, sifted
2-3 tablespoons boiling water
holly for decoration

1 Preheat a moderate oven (180 deg C, 350 deg F, Gas 4), centre shelf. Grease a 20 cm (8in) round cake tin and line with greased greaseproof paper.

2 Rub butter into flour until mixture resembles fine crumbs. Add the brown sugar, orange and lemon rind.

3 Beat the eggs with the brandy or milk.

4 Make a well in the centre of the rubbed-in mixture, add the eggs and mincemeat. Mix well.

5 Turn the mixture into the tin and spread evenly. Bake for 2 hours or until a warm skewer inserted in the centre comes out clean. Remove the cake from the tin and cool on a wire rack. Remove the greaseproof paper when the cake is cold.

6 Roll out the almond past to a round 10 cm (4in) wider then the diameter of the cake. Heat the apricot jam in a small pan until boiling hot. Brush the cake all over with the hot jam. Carefully lift the almond paste on to the cake; press firmly but gently in place over the top and down the side of the cake. Trim excess paste from round the base.

7 Put the cake on a wire rack and place over a large plate. Mix the icing sugar with 2-3 tablespoons boiling water to make a smooth icing, thick enough to coat the back of a wooden spoon evenly. Pour the icing directly into the centre of the cake, spread until it reaches the edge, then let it trickle down the side. Leave the cake on a wire rack overnight until completely set.

8 Lift on to a board or serving plate. Decorate the cake with holly leaves (or a decoration of your own choice).

Note: *This is a very quick and economical cake. It can be baked and iced all in one day, and is not too rich.*

CHRISTMAS GIFT CAKES

(Makes 9)

175 g (6oz) butter or margarine
175 g (6oz) castor sugar
3 eggs, beaten
175 g (6oz) self-raising flour
grated rind 1 orange or lemon, or ½ level teaspoon mixed spice
almond paste (see recipe on page 81)
yellow and orange food colourings
apricot glaze (see recipe on page 81)
coloured or silver ball cake decorations or chocolate drops (optional)

1 Preheat a moderately hot oven (190 deg C, 375 deg F, Gas 5), shelf above centre. Line the bases of two 18 cm (7in) square sandwich tins with non-stick paper.

2 Cream the butter and sugar until light and fluffy. Gradually beat in the eggs, beating thoroughly after each addition.

3 Fold in the flour and chosen flavouring. Turn into the prepared tins and smooth the tops.

4 Bake for 20-25 minutes until well risen and cooked through. Cool on a wire rack.

5 Cut off three-quarters of the almond paste and knead in yellow colouring. Knead orange colouring into remainder.

6 Trim the tops of the cakes to level the surface. Sandwich together with apricot glaze. Brush the top with more apricot glaze.

7 Roll out a piece of the yellow almond paste to about 6 mm (¼in) thick. Put the cake, glazed side down, on to the

almond paste and press down lightly. Trim the almond paste to the size of the cake. Using a large knife, cut the cake into 9 squares and transfer to a tray.

8 Roll out the remaining yellow almond paste to about 6 mm (¼in) thick. Cut into 9 strips about 5 cm (2in) wide (the depth of the cakes) by about 20 cm (8in) long (to go round the sides of the cakes). Brush the strips with apricot glaze. Put each cake on its side at the end of a strip of paste and press this round the cake to cover evenly. Pinch joins lightly to seal and shape into neat squares using a palette knife. Place to one side.

9 Thinly roll out the orange almond paste into an oblong and cut into 18 strips about 6 mm (¼in) wide. Brush the strips with apricot glaze and arrange two on each cake to represent ribbon. Press down lightly and trim ends.

10 If liked, cut and form remaining orange almond paste into loops to make bows for tops of cakes. Stick in position, using apricot glaze. If liked, decorate bows with coloured or silver ball decorations or chocolate drops.

11 Allow the cakes to set, before storing in an airtight container. They keep well for up to a week. Wrap in polythene if giving away as a present.

CHRISTMAS SHORTBREAD

(Makes 8 pieces)

50 g (2oz) glacé cherries
25 g (1oz) angelica
25 g (1oz) blanched almonds
100 g (4oz) butter
50 g (2oz) castor sugar
150 g (6oz) plain flour

1 Preheat a cool oven (150 deg C, 300 deg F, Gas 2), centre shelf. Grease a 23 cm (9in) sandwich tin, or an 18 cm (7in) square tin, preferably with loose base.

2 Rinse and chop the cherries and angelica. Roughly chop the almonds.

3 Put the butter in a bowl and cream until soft and fluffy, add the sugar and beat well. Add the cherries, angelica, almonds and flour.

4 Knead the mixture together with your hands. Continue kneading until smooth.

5 Place on a floured surface. Roll out until nearly large enough to fill the prepared tin.

6 Lift the shortbread into the tin and spread with a knife to cover the base of the tin, smooth the top. Decorate the edge with the end of a knife, prick the centre with a fork, mark into pieces, if liked.

7 Bake for 35-45 minutes. If cutting into pieces, do this at once. Cool whole or cut shortbread on a wire rack.

chapter 11
No-bake Cakes and Biscuits

The cheesecakes and gâteaux you 'cook' in the fridge –
and the special crispies, crunchies and sweetmeats that
don't need an oven

CHEESECAKE WITH FRUIT

(Serves 12)
BISCUIT BASE
226 g (8oz) packet digestive biscuits
75 g (3oz) butter
CHEESECAKE
227 g (8oz) packet full fat soft cheese
grated rind 1 lemon
½ teaspoon vanilla essence
3 eggs, separated
142 ml (5fl oz) carton soured cream
1 envelope gelatine
3 tablespoons hot water
75 g (3oz) castor sugar
FRUIT TOPPING
3-4 peaches, depending on size
lemon juice
1 small punnet redcurrants

1 Lightly oil a loose-based cake tin or spring-form pan,
about 20-23 cm (8-9in) diameter.
2 Place the digestive biscuits between 2 sheets of paper,
and crush with a rolling pin. Melt the butter in a
medium-sized pan and stir in the crumbs. Mix
thoroughly then turn into the cake tin. Spread evenly
over the base and press down. Chill.
3 Cream the cheese with the lemon rind and essence
then gradually beat in the egg yolks and soured cream.
4 Put the gelatine in a cup and add 3 tablespoons hot
water, allow to swell for a few minutes. Place in a pan of
hot water and stir until dissolved. Mix into the cream
cheese mixture.
5 Whisk the egg whites till stiff and standing in peaks
then gradually beat in the sugar. Fold this mixture into
the cheese mixture until evenly blended.
6 Pour into the biscuit lined tin and chill overnight.
7 To serve, dip the peaches into boiling water to loosen
the skin, then strip off the skins, cut in half and remove
the stones. Brush with lemon juice. Thoroughly wash,
drain and dry the redcurrants.
8 Run a round-bladed knife around the inside of the tin
and transfer the cake to a large serving dish.
9 Arrange the prepared fruits neatly over the top of the
cheesecake. Chill until required.
Note: *Strawberries, raspberries, loganberries, blackberries, etc,
could also be used.*

See picture opposite

FRESH RASPBERRY CHEESECAKE

(Serves 5-6)
BISCUIT CRUMB BASE
175 g (6oz) digestive biscuits
50 g (2oz) butter
25 g (1oz) castor sugar
FILLING
3 tablespoons very hot water
1 envelope gelatine
350 g (12oz) curd cheese
75 g (3oz) castor sugar
½ teaspoon vanilla essence
175 ml (6fl oz) double cream
2 egg whites
TO DECORATE
125 g (4oz) raspberries, hulled
castor sugar
a few small washed raspberry leaves or mint leaves

*It is important to follow **either** the metric **or** the imperial weights
and measures in any one recipe*

Cheesecake with Fruit, *see opposite*

SAUCE
225 g (8oz) raspberries, hulled
50 g (2oz) icing sugar

1 Butter a 19 cm (7½in) loose-based round cake tin.
2 Place the digestive biscuits in a bowl or large paper bag and crush with a rolling pin until quite fine.
3 Melt the butter in a pan. Stir in the biscuit crumbs and sugar so that all the butter is absorbed and the crumbs are coated.
4 Turn half the crumb mixture into the tin and, using the back of a spoon, press firmly to the base.
5 **To make the filling:** Place the hot water in a cup and sprinkle on the gelatine. Leave to dissolve (if necessary stand the cup in a saucepan of hot water). Cool slightly.
6 Place the curd cheese, sugar and vanilla essence in a bowl; beat until smooth.
7 Softly whip the cream and fold into the mixture. Stiffly whisk the egg whites.
8 Pour in the gelatine, stirring all the time, then fold in the egg whites.
9 Pour the mixture over the biscuit base in the tin and smooth over the top with a palette knife.
10 Leave until almost set and cover evenly with remaining crumb mixture. Put into the refrigerator and leave until set.
11 **To decorate:** Remove the cheesecake from the tin by standing the base on an upturned jam jar and carefully loosening the sides. Carefully ease the cheesecake from the base, using a fish slice, and a palette knife. Place the cake on a serving dish.
12 Pile the raspberries in the centre of the cheesecake. Sprinkle with a little castor sugar and decorate with a few raspberry or mint leaves, if liked. (The cheesecake can be stored in a refrigerator for up to 2 days.)
13 **To make the sauce:** Place the raspberries in a bowl. Sift the icing sugar over the raspberries and crush with the back of a wooden spoon. Cover the raspberries, leave until the syrup begins to run, about 30 minutes. Place in an electric blender and switch on to make a purée. Pour into a nylon sieve and press through into a bowl to remove pips. Pour into a sauceboat or jug.
14 Serve the sauce with the cheesecake.

GATEAU LOUISE

(Cuts into 8 portions)
100 g (4oz) plain dessert chocolate
175 g (6oz) butter
175 g (6oz) castor sugar
1 teaspoon almond essence
100 g (4oz) ground almonds
100 g (4oz) cake crumbs
275 ml (½ pint) double cream, whipped
11 sponge finger biscuits
1 chocolate flake bar
blanched split almonds

1 Break the chocolate in pieces into a basin, standing over hot water, and leave until soft, then remove the basin from the heat so the chocolate cools slightly.

2 Cream the butter with the castor sugar until soft and fluffy. Mix in the almond essence, softened chocolate, ground almonds and cake crumbs. Work the ingredients evenly together.
3 Stir half the whipped cream into the chocolate almond mixture. Store remaining cream in a bowl covered with cling-film.
4 Grease a loose-based 15 cm (6in) round cake tin, turn the mixture into it. Smooth the top then tap the tin sharply to release any trapped air.
5 Press a piece of kitchen foil over the surface and leave in a cold place overnight until firm.
6 Slip a knife round the edge of the cake to loosen and turn out on to a flat serving plate.
7 Cut the sponge finger biscuits in half and press them firmly round the side of the cake with the sugared sides out. A bright coloured ribbon may be tied round if you have one.
8 Decorate the top with whipped cream, crumbled chocolate flake and blanched split almonds.

CRUMB CAKE MOCHA

(Cuts into 8 portions)
100 g (4oz) butter or margarine
2 level teaspoons instant coffee powder
25 g (1oz) castor sugar
1 rounded tablespoon golden syrup
50 g (2oz) walnuts, chopped
1 level tablespoon ground coffee
50 g (2oz) raisins, chopped
50 g (2oz) glacé cherries, chopped
226 g (8oz) packet of digestive biscuits, crumbed
100 g (4oz) icing sugar
1 teaspoon coffee essence
7 walnut halves to decorate

1 Cream the butter, coffee powder, sugar and syrup together until soft.
2 Stir the walnuts, ground coffee, raisins and glacé cherries into the coffee cream. Work in the biscuit crumbs.
3 Pat the crumbly mixture into a well greased 18 cm (7in) sandwich tin or flan ring standing on a baking sheet. Smooth over the top and leave aside in a cold place until it is set.
4 Work the icing sugar together with 3 teaspoons of water and the coffee essence to a smooth coating icing.
5 Turn the set cake out of the tin on to a serving plate, spread the coffee icing over. Decorate with the walnuts.

RUM TRUFFLE CAKES

(Makes 12)
75 g (3oz) soft margarine
75 g (3oz) icing sugar
25 g (1oz) cocoa
½ teaspoon (or more to taste) rum essence
175 g (6oz) cake crumbs (made from Madeira cake)
225 g (8oz) bought or home-made almond paste
extra cocoa for dusting

1 Cream the margarine with the sifted icing sugar, cocoa and rum essence.
2 Work the cake crumbs into the chocolate cream until evenly blended.
3 Divide the mixture into 12 equal-sized pieces and then shape into balls. Place in a cold place for about one hour, or until firm.
4 Divide the almond paste into 12 equal pieces and then roll each to a round about 10 cm (4in) in diameter.
5 Wrap each truffle ball in a round of almond paste, bringing the edges up to the top; lightly seal them together.
6 Dust each truffle cake fairly thickly with cocoa. Serve piled on a plate.

DATE AND CHOCOLATE CRUNCH

(Cuts into 10-12 wedges)
50 g (2oz) fresh brown breadcrumbs
175 g (6oz) plain digestive biscuits, roughly crushed
125 g (4oz) stoned dates, chopped
50 g (2oz) sultanas
113 g (4oz) packet chocolate drops for cooking
150 g (5oz) butter
1 rounded tablespoon thick honey

1 Place a 19 cm (7½in) fluted flan ring on a baking sheet and grease lightly.
2 Grill the breadcrumbs, turning frequently until really crisp and dry. Mix with the crushed biscuits, dates, sultanas and half the chocolate drops.
3 Melt 125 g (4oz) butter with the honey. Pour into the biscuit mixture, stir well until all the ingredients are coated. Turn into the flan ring, press down firmly and

smooth the surface. Leave until quite cold, then loosen and remove the flan ring.
4 Melt remaining 25 g (1oz) butter with the rest of the chocolate drops and a teaspoon hot water in a small bowl over a pan of hot water. Mix well and spread over the biscuit mixture then leave until set. Cut into wedges. Keeps well in an airtight container for up to 8 days.

CHOCOLATE BOX CAKE

(Cuts into 8 slices)
200 g (7.05oz) bar plain chocolate
142 ml (5fl oz) carton soured cream
2 packets sponge layers (unfilled)
a few walnut halves
glacé cherries and angelica to decorate

1 Break the chocolate into small pieces and put into a small basin. Place over a saucepan of hot water. Leave until the chocolate melts.
2 Remove from the heat, stir with a round-bladed knife until smooth. Stir in the soured cream. Allow to cool a little until the mixture becomes thick and heavy.
3 Sandwich all 6 sponge layers together with one third of the chocolate mixture.
4 Turn the cake on its side so that the sponge layers stand vertically. Place on a flat serving plate. Completely cover the cake with the rest of the chocolate mixture, marking it into swirls, or peaks.
5 Decorate the top with walnuts, glacé cherries and angelica.
6 Refrigerate the cake until the icing sets.

GINGER CRISPIES

(Makes 12)
75 g (3oz) butter or hard margarine
2 level teaspoons golden syrup
1 level teaspoon ground ginger
50 g (2oz) soft brown sugar
1 tablespoon creamy milk
75 g (3oz) rice cereal
pieces of stem ginger (optional)

1 Place 12 paper cake cases in the hollows of tartlet tins or on a baking sheet.
2 Gently heat all the ingredients, except the cereal and stem ginger, until the sugar dissolves. Boil 3 minutes to make a butterscotch, taking care not to let the mixture boil over.
3 Remove from heat. Add the cereal and mix thoroughly
4 Using two spoons, divide the mixture between the paper cases, piling it up and pressing together lightly.
5 If using ginger, dip into any butterscotch mix left in pan, press into the top of the crispies. Leave to cool and set. Best eaten quickly.

See picture on page 55

LEMON AND PINEAPPLE GATEAU

(Serves 6-8)

150 g (5oz) butter or soft margarine
75 g (3oz) icing sugar
2 egg yolks
finely grated rind and juice 1 lemon
341 g (12oz) can small pineapple rings
24 sponge finger biscuits
few pieces angelica for decoration

1 Cream the butter with the icing sugar until light and fluffy, beat in the egg yolks. Stir in the lemon rind.
2 Drain the juice from the pineapple, finely chop half the rings and stir them into half the lemon cream.
3 Measure 150 ml (5fl oz) of the juice from the pineapple, stir in the lemon juice.
4 Place 8 of the sponge finger biscuits side by side on a plate and sprinkle them with a third of the pineapple and lemon juice.
5 Spread half the chopped pineapple and lemon cream over the biscuits.
6 Arrange 2 rows of biscuits (4 to each row) at right angles on top of first layer.
7 Sprinkle these biscuits with another third of the juice, spread with remaining pineapple and lemon cream.
8 Arrange a final layer of biscuits on top similar to the bottom layer, sprinkle with remaining juice, spread half the plain lemon butter cream smoothly over top.
9 Cover the cake and place it aside for 24 hours to allow the pineapple and lemon flavours to combine and moisten the biscuits.
10 If liked, trim the sides of the gâteau with a sharp knife. Arrange the remaining pineapple slices down the centre and pipe or spoon the remaining lemon butter cream either side. Decorate the edge with angelica.
See picture below

RUM AND COFFEE CAKE

(Serves 8-12)

75 g (3oz) ground hazelnuts
50 ml (2fl oz) milk
75 g (3oz) butter
75 g (3oz) icing sugar, sifted
1 egg, beaten
250 ml (½ pint) cold strong black coffee made from ground or instant coffee
1 tablespoon rum
about 36 sponge finger biscuits

Lemon and Pineapple Gâteau, *see above*

COATING
150 ml (5fl oz) double cream
few drops vanilla essence
sugar to taste
few whole hazelnuts for decoration

1 Put the ground hazelnuts in a small bowl and cover with hot milk. Leave to cool. Grease an 18 cm (7in) round loose-based cake tin.
2 Cream the butter then gradually beat in the icing sugar, beating well until light and fluffy. Beat in the egg and then the cold hazelnut mixture.
3 Pour the coffee and rum into a shallow dish. Dip the sponge fingers, one at a time, into the mixture and arrange over the base of the prepared tin, breaking biscuits as necessary. Spread with half the nut mixture.
4 Repeat the coffee biscuit and nut mixture layers and top with a third layer of coffee biscuit.
5 Grease the base of a plate which will fit into the tin, place this on the mixture and put a weight on top. Chill overnight.
6 **To make coating:** Whisk the cream with the essence and sugar, until stiff enough to hold its shape.
7 **To serve:** Ease the cake from the tin on to a serving plate. Spread the sides and top with the cream and, if liked, decorate with nuts.

See picture below

APRICOT SWEETMEATS

(Makes 30)
125 g (4oz) dried apricots, soaked overnight
1 small orange, well washed
125 g (4oz) granulated sugar
75 g (3oz) desiccated coconut

1 Soak the apricots in 150 ml (5fl oz) water overnight. Put the apricots in a pan.
2 Make the water up to 250 ml (½ pint), add to pan and cook the apricots until tender.
3 Cook the whole orange in water until tender. Drain. Cut in half and remove pips.
4 Put both fruits through a fine mincer or Mouli grinder and place in the top of a double saucepan. Add the sugar.
5 Cook until the mixture is thick and sets when tested by placing a small sample on a saucer in refrigerator.
6 Set aside until cold. Chill.
7 Shape into 30 small balls, roll in coconut and chill.

Rum and Coffee Cake, *see opposite*

CHOCOLATE AND ORANGE CRUNCH

(Cuts into 6-8 wedges)
175 g (6oz) milk chocolate
125 g (4oz) peanut butter
25 g (1oz) butter or margarine
175 g (6oz) rich Osborne biscuits
1 orange
50 g (2oz) chopped mixed peel
25 g (1oz) seedless raisins
150 ml (5fl oz) double cream

1 Break the chocolate into a medium-sized saucepan. Add the peanut butter, and butter or margarine. Heat gently to just melt the chocolate, but do not allow to get too hot.
2 Break the biscuits into fairly small pieces, stir into the chocolate.
3 Thinly peel two strips rind from the orange, finely grate the remainder. Add the grated rind, mixed peel and raisins to the chocolate mixture.
4 Press the mixture into a lightly oiled 15-18 cm (6-7in) cake tin. Chill until firm, then turn out.
5 Whisk the cream until softly stiff, pipe a design on top. Cut the orange rind into thin shreds and arrange on the cream. Serve cut in wedges.

Note: *This should be served the day it is made. It needs to be cut carefully.*

GINGERNUT CHOCOLATE CAKE

(Cuts into 8-10 slices)
200 g (7.05oz) packet gingernuts
200 g (8oz) butter
200 g (7.05oz) packet chocolate cake covering
2 eggs, separated
2 tablespoons single cream
DECORATION
2 pieces crystallised or preserved ginger, sliced

1 Oil a 15-18 cm (7-8in) round cake tin and line with oiled greaseproof paper.
2 Break or cut the gingernuts into 6-12 mm ($\frac{1}{4}$-$\frac{1}{2}$in) pieces.
3 Put the butter in a small pan over a gentle heat until half melted. Place on one side.
4 Break the chocolate into small pieces and place in a bowl that will fit over a pan of hot, not boiling water. Allow the chocolate to melt.
5 Remove chocolate from heat, beat in the egg yolks and then gradually beat in the butter.
6 Whisk the egg whites until stiff and standing in peaks. Fold into the chocolate mixture until evenly mixed.
7 Add the single cream and gingernut pieces and fold into the mixture.
8 Turn into the prepared tin. Chill for at least 2 hours, or overnight.

9 **To serve:** Carefully ease from the tin, remove the paper, place the cake on a serving dish and decorate the top with ginger slices. It is best eaten with a fork.
Note: *This cake is very rich, but, if liked, it could be served coated with whipped cream.*

CHOCOLATE CRUNCH

(Cuts into 6 pieces)
2 Mars bars
50 g (2oz) butter
1 egg
25 g (1oz) nuts and raisins
8 digestive biscuits, crushed

1 Cut the bars into pieces and put in a basin. Stand it in a saucepan of boiling water until the chocolate has melted. Stir in the butter.
2 Separate the yolk and white of the egg. Stir the yolk into the mixture. Stiffly whisk the white and fold in. Stir in the nuts and raisins and the biscuits.
3 Place in a greased 18 cm (7in) round sandwich tin and spread evenly. Leave in a cool place to set.
4 Just before serving, cut into 6 pieces. Serve with cream.

Index